Cover photo:
"He often raised his eyes to the sky as if he could see something or as if he was talking to somebody"

Printed by:
Grafiche GRILLI srl – Foggia (Italy)
Via Manfredonia Km 2,200

To the Prayer groups
born from the heart of Padre Pio
may they treasure his memory
and act in the world as ferment
of Christian life.

FIRST PART

"*His mission to save souls*",
Testimonies; year 2006

THIRD PART

"*The great family under the protection of Our Lady*".
Testimonies; year 2008

Fr. Marcellino IasenzaNiro

THE "PADRE"
SAINT PIO OF PIETRELCINA

Charismatic priest

Testimonies

SECOND PART

EDIZIONI

PADRE PIO
DA PIETRELCINA

Piazzale Santa Maria delle Grazie, 4
71013 San Giovanni Rotondo (FG) Italy 2015

Original title: "Il Padre" San Pio da Pietrelcina
"Sacerdote Carismatico - Testimonianze" anno 2006

Translated into English
by Patricia Anne Mackinlay

1st edition 2007
reprint 2010
reprint 2015

For additional copies of this book write to:
Edizioni "Padre Pio da Pietrelcina"
Piazzale Santa Maria delle Grazie, 4
71013 San Giovanni Rotondo (FG)-Italy

or contact :
The Voice of Padre Pio: Tel. +39 0882 418320/418305
Fax +39 0882 418327
Website: www.vocedipadrepio.com
e-mail: thevoice@vocedipadrepio.com

CONTENTS

IV. A FATHER'S HEART

INTRODUCTION

Dear reader, you have had the chance to read the first volume of the book *"The Padre"*. It was written by one of our confrères, to let people know more about Padre Pio a minister of God who had been entrusted with, the specific task of his life, *"the mission to save souls"*.

As you have probably noticed, the author of that book more than lingering to consider the Saint's work, preferred to talk to those who came close to this man of God and, through his help distanced themselves from sin. Today many of them live in the eternal happiness of Heaven, or deeply hope to reach it.

This *second* volume wishes to illustrate two aspects of Padre Pio's apostolic works:

1. the extraordinary help he received from the Holy Spirit. As the people who went to his confessional were numerous, God's servant needed the continual intervention of the Paraclete Spirit. We can realise through these pages how Padre Pio was a great charismatic, so much so that he could touch those near to him and be felt by those far away.

2. how much "heart" the Saint put into his care of souls. His hardness in reproving sinners to bring them back to the straight narrow path has been underlined too easily.

Here one can realise his efficacious love for his spiritual children who accepted his invitation to live by God's rules and put their trust in him.

We are sure you will welcome and enjoy these pages as much as you did whilst reading volume I.

San Giovanni Rotondo 29 June 2007.

PADRE PIO

CHARISMATIC PRIEST

III. THE GIFTS OF THE SOUL

P. Pio's apostolic work, carried out mainly in the confessional, was always accompanied by clear signs of the intervention of God's goodness, who through this faithful servant of His, soothed the ills of souls and bodies of his children.

Now we wish to examine more carefully the gifts the Holy Spirit gave to his servant, gifts suitable to help him carry out his mission.

Introduction

Pope Pius XII says that the Holy Spirit is the "beginning of every vital and redeeming action in each limb of the Mystical Body" of Christ, that is in each Christian.

Without his action we, from a spiritual point of view are dead. As St Augustine rightly observed: "What our soul is for our limbs, the Holy Spirit is for Christ's limbs".

The third person of the Holy Trinity normally works in the Church through the Word of God that "has the power to build one up", the Sacraments which make us grow and heal, and the virtues which make us act according to what is good.[1]

However the Vatican Council II points out: "The Holy Spirit, not only sanctifies God's people, guides them and adorns

---

[1] Cfr. Catechismo…, n. 798.

them with virtues, through sacraments and ministries, but by *"apportioning to each one individually as He wills"* (1Cor 12, 11), also gives out among faithful of each order special gifts, with which he makes them suitable and ready to take on various works and duties, useful to renew and expand the Church, according to those words: *"To each is given the manifestation of the Spirit for the common good"* (1Cor, 12, 7)[2].

According to the Council text, there are two privileged channels which the Holy Spirit uses in his actions aimed at sanctifying God's people: the sacraments and charisms.

The first arrive to us through hierarchy.

In fact, Jesus said to the apostles: *"Go ye therefore and teach all nations baptizing them in the name of the Father and of the Son and of the Holy Spirit"* (Mt 28, 19); and he gave them the power to give back grace to the sinners: *"Those who forgive sins shall be forgiven"* (Jh 20, 23); and he instituting the Eucharist gave them the task of giving the Church His body and His blood: *"Do this in memory of me"* (Lk 19, 22).

The charisms instead, a particular manifestation of the Spirit, are not given to a certain category or order, but as the apostle himself says, *"to every one"* (1 Cor 12, 11), as the Spirit, that *"blows where it wishes"* (cfr. Jh 3, 8), offers just "as he likes" his grace to the "single cells" of the Mystic Body.

It must be added that these charisms do not sanctify those who receive them, that is why they are called *"gratiae gratis datae"* and by the person chosen by the Spirit, they must be *"employed for one another"*, as Peter teaches us (1 Pt 4, 10). And Paul points out that they are given to *"enable the brothers*

---

[2]   *Lumen Gentium…*, 12.

to carry out the work of ministry in order to build up the body of Christ". (Ep 4, 11).

We can summarize that: "the sacraments are the gift given to all to be useful to everyone; the charism are gifts given to individual people, to sanctify the Church as a whole".

Father Raniero Cantalamessa notes: "It is easy to understand what a loss it would be for the Church, if, at a certain point, one thought to do without one of the two channels, either sacraments or charisms or of the Holy Spirit from above, from the steps of the hierarchy of the Spirit that is diffused at the base of the Church. Now, unfortunately, we must say that such a thing did happen in the Church at least at a practical level if not as a principle. After the Second Vatican Council everyone acknowledged that in the past there had been a certain reduction in the sanctifying organism of the Church with regards to the charisms".[3]

Rightly enough the above quoted Council text declares: "These charisms, extraordinary ones and even more simple and ordinary ones, must be accepted with gratitude and consolation because they are useful and necessary to the Church".[4]

Saint Paul in his letter to the Corinthians opens one to the truth of this treasure: *"There are a variety of gifts…; to one is given through the Spirit the utterance of wisdom, and to another the utterance of knowledge according to the same Spirit, to another faith, to another the gift of healing, to another the working of miracles, to another prophecy, to another the abil-*

---

[3]   R. CANTALAMESSA, *Rinnovarsi nello Spirito*, Ed Paoline 1984, 112.

[4]   *Lumen Gentium* n. 12.

ity to distinguish between spirits, to another the interpretation of tongues" (1 Cor 12,4).

The same apostle then in his letter to the Romans talks about gifts regarding the serving, the teaching, the exhortation or the gift of *"he who gives"*, of *"he who presides"*, of *"he who does act of mercy"* (cfr. Rm, 7-8).

Who receives charismas

It has been said that charismas do not bring an increase in sanctifying grace: they are given to bring benefit to others, not to enrich those who receive them.

Our confrère Fr Raniero writes: "It is true that the charism is not given due to sanctity or in view of the sanctity of a person, but it is also true that it does not stay wholesome if it is not based on personal holiness".[5]

The gift of the Spirit must be jealously guarded by whoever receives it by meticulously observing Christian virtues, three in particular: obedience to the Church, humility and charity towards others.

With regards to the first virtue the Vatican Council II, in the afore quoted document states: "The judgement of their genuine and meticulous use belongs to the Ecclesiastical Authorities, whose task is to examine all and judge what is good, and especially not to extinguish the Spirit" (L.G. n.12; cfr. Ts 5,12. 19-21).

---

[5]   R. CANTALAMESSA, *Il canto dello Spirito*, Ed. Ancona 1997, 195.

Padre Pio, a charismatic Saint

It has been rightly said that P. Pio is one of the greatest mystics of the church, and charismatic like few others. All those who lived near the Padre felt that he had been enriched with extraordinary gifts from God.

It was a widespread opinion that the Saint could read one's conscience and to receive advice from him was considered a fortune, because his word was prophetic, that is truthful and therefore reassuring. It has already been observed that in case of sickness, the touch of his hand could cure.

It we look at the list of charisms that St. Paul gives us, we can see that a large number of them were exercised by the Padre. One should not be surprised by this abundance of special graces given to him by the Spirit.

Every Saint has a special task from God to carry out on earth. Each faithful servant is gifted by the Lord with the necessary means to carry out what has been established by the Divine Providence. Each Saint experiences what has happened to Jesus.

Cantalamessa writes: "The personal identity of Jesus in the Gospels can be seen from two fundamental relationships: that of Son in relationship to his Father, characterized by obedience, and that with the Spirit, from which comes authority, freedom and power of his mission. The charismatic Spirit confers the Messiah's anointment to take the Gospel to the poor and to heal broken hearts with which he drives away demons, which makes him "brim over" with joy in prayer, it is not an accessory in Jesus' mission, but is constitutive.

Also in the life of the first Christian community the charisms were not private facts, an extra or a luxury, but they were that which, together with the apostolic authority, outlined the character of the community.[6]

We know that the mission assigned to P. Pio by the Lord was not confined or bound to a parish, a region or a nation. Even though he spent the largest part of his life in the friary of San Giovanni Rotondo, hundreds and thousands of people from all over the world were drown to him.

Especially because of the gift of the stigmata his crucified image was lifted up between Heaven and Earth, so that it could be seen, observed and admired. Perhaps it was also discussed but it was always disquieting for what the friar was and indicated.

As the mission of the crucified friar of the Gargano was worldwide, a special assistance was needed from God, who had given him this mission. This explains the active presence of the Holy Spirit, the Counsellor, the Paraclete as defined by Jesus, that is he who when "called in help" intervenes (cfr. Jh 14, 24).

1. Searching one's soul

According to St Thomas Aquinas, the gift of being able to read one's soul is a grace through which a holy man, delving into the depth of a person's heart can see and show hidden things that only God and that person's conscience know. [7]

Scaramelli, one of the most illustrious masters of spirituality, examining this particular gift, specifies: "There is no doubt that this gift has some time been given by God to his faithful servants.

---

[6]   Ibid. 199.

[7]   TOMMASO D'AQUINO, Summa Teologica 1.2 q III. Art. 4.

Some whilst carrying out the sacrament of confession un-
covered to the penitents, sins that they had forgotten to confess
due to a bad memory or because of guilty embarrassment. A
clear sign that they managed to look into the intimate part of
the penitent's consciences.

Others managed to see in what state the souls of others
were, in grace: this is a higher and more valuable level of dis-
cretion".[8]

This charism in both aspects indicated by the learned man,
was present in P. Pio's life.

P. Pio sees the state of the soul in sin and admonishes

It has been noted above in which way the Holy Spirit aided
P. Pio while he administered the sacrament of Penance, and
almost always opens to his faithful servant the vision of the
penitent's soul, in order that the sacrament is more efficient.

But one can affirm that during the various daily actions of
the Lord's servant, working for the good of his brethren are
immersed in the same light of the Spirit and supported by His
force.

For P. Pio every occasion was right to call back souls to be
converted.

Here are some cases:
1. A lady tells us: "I had to leave for San Giovanni Rotondo

---

[8]   G. BATTISTA SCARAMELLI, Dottrina di S. Giovanni della Croce
e discernimento degli spiriti, Ed. Pia Società di S. Paolo, Roma 1946,
246.

where I had booked a confession with the Padre. I had looked up the time of the trains, when unexpectedly my husband offered to take me by car.

When I arrived in the Gargano I gave up the booking I had to confess and asked a friar if he could arrange a meeting with P. Pio instead. I hoped that his presence alone and one of his looks would be able to make my husband mend his ways and leave his libertine lifestyle full of continual unfaithfulness. Our request was granted and we were put in the corridor where the Saint would pass by.

P. Pio arrived shortly and looking at my husband who was at my side said to him: "What are you waiting for to turn over a new leaf, are you waiting for your wife to tell you to?"[9]

2. "My brother Giuseppe", another lady told us, "had left his wife and children and gone to Congo where he lived an immoral life.

Once, when he was back in Italy, as he was in Puglia, he went up to San Giovanni Rotondo to see P. Pio, whom he had often heard his father, who had met him, speak of.

He went into the Church and when the Saint had finished confessing, he joined a group of men who pressed around the Saint. He got as near to him as possible but was behind his back.

At a certain point P. Pio turned round and said to him: "Go away, you have the stink of sin about you".[10]

3. A fellow had a soft spot for a woman from San Giovanni Rotondo and every so often with the excuse of seeing P. Pio he came to the town and stayed longer than he should.

---

[9]   I.C., Chiavari 3.10.1995.
[10] L.C., Thiene, 23.5.1998, 10.00 a.m.

One day the Padre, seeing him among the men who waited on the wings as he had his walk down the corridor, said to him: "What are you doing here at San Giovanni Rotondo?".

"I'm keeping my sister who married a man from here company".

And the Saint: "And where do you come in? Your sister has to stay with her husband. You go and keep your father who is ill company".

When he returned home he found his father seriously ill in bed.[11]

4. "Young Lino De Pieri, from Padova, came close to P. Pio to be blessed but the Padre looked at him and ordered: "Take the communist membership card out of your wallet together with the photographs of those filthy women you keep so jealously. Don't you feel ashamed carrying those photos?".

"Yes", answered the youth trembling.

"And, since you are determined to have a clean out, now that you return home, tear up all those indecent things you keep in the table drawer".[12]

5. Sometimes a meeting with the Saint could be traumatic and then become a beneficial moment, in which the destiny of a soul could be decided for eternity.

One day P. Pio after finishing the women's confession in the church, went back to the friary with Fr Tarcisio Zullo from Cervinara, who gave him his arm to lessen the exertion of

---

[11]   San Giovanni Rotondo, May 1993.
[12]   Chronicle of the Friary, ff. 391-392: 3 February 1955.

climbing the stairs. They rested on the landing where there is the picture that invites one to pray for the Souls in Purgatory, and he stopped to pray for a few moments.[13]

At that moment Mr Giuseppe Pezzini from Bologna approached him and said: "Father, I wish to confess".

And the Saint after looking at him with those eyes of his which penetrated deep into the soul, answered: "Can't you seen how blackened your soul is?"

"Yes Father, but I must have done some good in my life!".

P. Pio replied: "Your goodness is like the glow-worms that appear once in a blue moon and that need a dark night to be seen. Go home and come back in three months time and I will confess you". But after a pause he warned: "Be prepared to suffer".

Giuseppe, when the two friars moved away, refused to accept these harsh words he was not accustomed to. As he travelled a lot and often went down to Puglia, his family had advised him to stop to see that that extraordinary saintly friar. They had told him it wouldn't have cost him anything. Instead he'd had a good telling off.

He left San Giovanni Rotondo with the intention of never returning, but when he reached Bologna he started to be tormented by the friar's parting expression: "Be prepared to suffer". What did he mean by this? His wonderings stopped when a check-up at the doctors discovered throat cancer and were replaced by a deep state of anxiety.

---

[13] In San Giovanni Rotondo, on the second floor of the friary stairs, there is a framed board with this heading: "Simple method to pray for the souls in Purgatory". In it are listed one hundred categories of people one can pray for. Each category is given a number , which is extracted from a little urn or box, by whoever passes. Padre Pio was very scrupulous in stopping and in taking a number to see which souls he should pray to Heaven for.

However he remembered that Padre Pio's tone of voice, when he hinted at the future, was fatherly. Hadn't he also invited him to return?

Giuseppe returned to the Saint who comforted him and put him back in God's grace after a good healthy confession.

He seemed a changed man: he became humble and put all his trust in P. Pio who became his spiritual father.

When he went back home he had to undergo an operation. It seemed as if all was going well but after a few years the doctors advised a fresh operation as the illness had grown acute again.

By now he had become familiar with the Padre and didn't make a move without consulting him. He did so in this occasion too and the Saint's opinion was completely against that of the surgeon. "They will only take away your vocal chords. Now stay away from the operating table".

When the poor patient told the head physician what P. Pio had said, his answer was: "Tell your protector to act like a friar not a doctor". However Pezzini listened to the Padre and refused to be touched by the doctors. As the years went by the patient observed that all his friends suffering from the same illness who had undergone a further operation had died. He was serene and said to one and all: "P. Pio has already given me a few extra years, what else do I want?".

He often went down to San Giovanni Rotondo. But the illness continued. In the final stage he was sent to the Mangiagalli Clinic in Milan where the capuchin friars went each morning to celebrate Mass, and visiting the various departments brought relief to the sick patient by giving them Communion.

I too for a period was one of them and through Fr. Tarcisio Zullo I used to inform the Saint about the illness of his spiritual son. The Padre sent continual messages of sweet relief.

Comforted in this way Giuseppe ended his painful calvary that Padre Pio had foreseen.[14]

Fr. Gerardo Di Flumeri in a conference held about our Saint in a Capuchin Friary in Cerignola (FG) speaking of the charism which allowed him to read people's conscience, defined this as a "terrible power".[15]

That what the confrère pointed out is true can be seen in a particular way by the following testimony.

One day in February 1958 (or '59) a retired ex Army General, Tosi from Voghera, came to San Giovanni Rotondo to meet P. Pio.

The air was icy cold. Taking the road to go up to the friary, he had difficulty in moving forwards because the gale force wind caught his breath. After half an hour of sufferings he arrived at the courtyard of the little shrine of Our Lady of Graces and caught sight of a friar's shadow. It was P. Pio who was waiting for him at the threshold of the church.

The Saint let him come in, so that he could shelter and pointing to the whirling snow which joined the sky to the ground said: "Look at them, look them in the face. Your soldiers! You had them all shot down, you did!".

Shocked, unable to say a single word, as if swallowed up he found himself once more in the snowstorm. As he went away the wind blew away his hat but a woman picked it up. "Shall we go down together?", she asked as she gave him back his hat.

---

[14] Fr. Tarcisio Zulla from Cervinara, Campobasso 21.10.1985.

[15] Cfr. Fr. Gerardo Di Flumeri, I carismi di Padre Pio, in Padre Pio da Pietrelcina . Approdo a Dio degli uomini del secolo ventesimo, edited by P. Bonaventura Massa, Convento Santa Maria delle Grazie Ed., San Giovanni Rotondo 1981, 72.

Comforted by this kindly person he gave her his arm and felt the need to open his heart to her.

He told her about his upsetting meeting with P. Pio and his harsh reproach. "I", he said "was only the president of the court. There was the Prosecutor, there was the jury, there were serious charges of desertion and other crimes". And he spoke and spoke as if to shake off that sentence he had received a little while before from the Saint. He was extremely upset.

When the two of them neared the Hotel, the General thanked the kind woman who had kept him company and added: "I'm getting my suitcase and leaving…feeling desperate!".

He went to his room, collected his few personal things and asked the porter to call him a taxi, which arrived quickly. He got in and shouted to the driver: "Foggia, the railway Station". The driver went down the "viale Cappuccini" road, entered into town and then at the cross road instead of turning right for Foggia, went straight on in the direction of Monte Sant'Angelo.

When he arrived in front of the cemetery gates the taxi driver stopped and said: "Here you are, you've arrived. You may get out".

"I asked you to take me to Foggia" shouted the general who was used to being instantly obeyed.

"Yes, but you have arrived", replied the driver very calmly.

The man upset and disturbed stopped himself. In the voice of the driver whose face he couldn't see, he heard the voice tone and accent of P. Pio. After a few moments silence he said: "Take me back to the hotel, I beg you".

The driver obeyed.

The general after being given his room key again in the reception hall, went up to his room where he began to think about his life.

He decided to stay longer.

The next morning, in the intense cold, he went once more to the friary and heard P. Pio's Mass. Then he joined the line of a few men who were waiting to confess. He was the last in line and the Padre gave him a lot of his precious time. Peace filled his heart.

After a few years he decided to build a little house to be able to enjoy, at least periodically the great gift that was P. Pio's presence.[16]

Scaramelli is right then, when speaking of the gift of "reading one's soul" to affirm that "there is nothing that can conciliate belief in faith's doctrine as much as seeing that he who proposes it wakes the mysteries of the heart which are evident only to God".[17]

a) Spiritual direction and searching

P. Pio used this gift from the Holy Spirit not only to rouse one from grave sinfulness but also to spiritually lead souls.

Regarding this Scaramelli writes: "There is nothing that leads the souls of their faithful in the right direction as penetrating the secret hiding places of their hearts.[18]

1. Enzo Picciafuoco tells us: "I wanted to find a good Christian framework to my life. I had had this thought in my mind for a while and I decided to talk to the Padre in confession.

---

[16]   Guerino Colosso, San Giovanni Rotondo 20.6.1998.
[17]   SCARAMELLI, Dottrina…, 246.
[18]   Ibid.

"Father, I'd like…"

He stopped me in mid speech and said: "Christian life should be based both on fear and love. Fear alone would take away enthusiasm and action, love alone, without restrain would lead one to taking advantages".[19]

2. P. Pio gave Mario Tentori reassuring comfort and filled him with peacefulness.

He was about to leave for San Giovanni Rotondo when he was filled with a strong violent temptation; but with the help of prayer and the thought that the day afterwards he would have met and re-embraced the Padre, he restrained from sinning.

When he approached the confessional to speak to P. Pio, the first thing he wanted to point out was that difficult moment when he was near to offending God; but the Padre, as soon as he opened his mouth said: "But you didn't do it!"

And the Saint knowing that his spiritual son was a scrupulous type, explained that a rejected temptation is not a sin but a reason for reward.[20]

3. Sister Pura Pagani instead was sternly called by the Padre to a stricter adherence of the rules a nun should follow.

She tells us: "Once when I was in Tarquinia, I had some troubles with my health so I decided to go to see P. Pio to talk to him about it. After saving some money I left with another sister.

When I arrived in San Giovanni Rotondo I begged Fr. Raffaele from Sant'Elia a Pianisi, who I knew, to help me meet the Padre. The good friar let me stand near to the confessional and

---

[19] Enzo Picciafuoco, Campobasso 22.7.1989.
[20] Father Bruno Borelli, Erba 19.9.1998.

at the moment the Saint finished listening to a penitent, pushed me towards him, but as soon as the Padre saw me he shouted: "Go away, go away!"

I felt hurt, because the Padre has always been so kind to me on previous meetings. I shrank back, dying with shame and stayed frozen in my place even after the Padre had finished confessing everyone and all tried to get near him to kiss his hand.

When on his way back to the sacristy, passing by the balustrade which delimited the area of the main altar, he nodded to a woman to call me to come closer to him. I only moved after the third call, I was afraid of being shouted at again.

As I got near to him he reassured me saying: "Keep calm, you'll feel better, you'll see, you'll feel better". Then as if to explain the reason of his severity he added: "But next time come when you have permission from your superiors".

The Padre had read my mind: I had not informed the Mother Superior fearing she would not allow me to go".[21]

Sister Pura was called upon by the Padre in another moment to mortify her curiosity and to live her meeting with Jesus, bread of the soul, more intimately.

She says: "In a visit to San Giovanni Rotondo, I had the privilege of receiving communion during holy Mass and as P. Pio had no gloves on, I tried to see his wounds. I heard him say: "Think about what you are doing".[22]

4. In 1951 Mario Sanci had a serious eye-problem. He was a student and feared that from one moment to the next he would be unable to study. He was told that to gain grace it was necessary to "assault the heart of Jesus".

---

[21] Sister Pura Pagani, Mozzecane (VR) 10.5.1997.

[22] Ibid.

He misunderstood the "assault" necessary to gain the Lords grace which is continuous prayer without stopping in the faith or certainty that nothing is impossible for him, whilst waiting in absolute humility like a poor man in need.

He wrote a letter to P. Pio speaking of this problem, ending with the words: "Father, from God I expect the blessing of good sight".

Much later he decided to go personally to San Giovanni Rotondo to ask in person his written request to P. Pio. The day after his arrival, finding himself in the sacristy he saw P. Pio for the first time, who passing close by him, with a gentle voice said: "But what do you expect, what do you expect?"[23]

5. Father Pasquale Cattaneo confessed to P. Pio, who encouraged him to try and overcome a spiritual difficulty, promising he would help him. The same day he found himself able to carry out the Padre's exhortation to have faith in his personal strength together with God's grace. He worked diligently overcoming obstacles with an ease he had never known before.

The next day he got up to the friary early to listen to the Padre's Mass, who soon after, in the sacristy gazing among the crowd picked him out and smiled to him. We know that P. Pio after Mass stayed absorbed in thanks. However for his spiritual son he wished to break his habit to confirm the validity of his advice as well as his continual assistance.

Father Cattaneo ended his testimony saying: "The Padre with that gaze told me clearly: "Have you seen I was right?""[24]

---

[23] Mario Sanci Salemi 2.11.1996.
[24] Father Pasquale Cattaneo, Fiera di Primiero (TN) 31.7.1988.

6. Our confrère brother Giovanni Sammarone tells us: "I worked in the kitchen of San Giovanni Rotondo and one afternoon in 1949, I was sent by Father Raffaele D'Addario to pick some chicory from the vegetable garden.

Whilst I was doing that I had a clear illumination from God with regards to my sins. I felt regret and repentance. I said to the Lord that I would rather die than commit one sin in the future. I left everything and went towards the church, but not finding a peaceful corner I went to the sacristy on the right of the benches where the priests dressed themselves for holy Mass.

Meanwhile P. Pio was confessing men. When he had finished despite being amongst all those people who gathered around him to touch or kiss his hand, he reached towards me and shook me strongly. I looked at him, but went back to my place.

On seeing this he took me again saying: "That's quite enough!! Now go and do what you have to do. The Lord has understood all you want to say".[25]

b) Reading of people's thought and affections

Part of the reading of souls is also the knowledge by God's men "to repeat with exactness one's thoughts and the affections nurtured in one's heart".[26]

The spiritual sons and daughters were convinced that nothing of their souls was hidden from the Padre.

---

[25]   Brother Giovanni Sammarone, Larino 9.9.1986.
[26]   SCARAMELLI, *Dottrina…*, 246.

Fr. Federico Carrozza, who in the years 1917-1920, in San Giovanni Rotondo, was a student of the little seraphic seminary where P. Pio was the spiritual director, gives this testimony: "I never witnessed anything extraordinary during my training period but I can say that all we students were convinced that P. Pio could read our minds".[27]

All we who have lived with the Padre can confirm what our confrère says. But apart from the experience that everyone sooner or later had being near the Saint, this conviction was confirmed by the Padre's own words.

One day in the square two women were having a heated discussion. One of them said: "The Padre knows all" and the other replied: "That's not possible".

A few days later she went to confession and before she started to speak she heard P. Pio say: "Through Jesus I hear all. I see all you do and hear all you say".[28]

And to the other spiritual daughter during a confession he said: "I can see your soul as you can see yourself in the mirror".[29]

1. Margherita Cassano, who was on friendly terms with the Padre, discovered in an unusual way that the Saint really could read her soul.

She says: "I confessed one Sunday to P. Pio who gave me a good telling off. I don't remember what for.

I left the confessional to go and do my penance but instead of examining my conscience, I prayed my special Saints to help me understand what the Padre wanted from me.

---

[27] Fr. Federico Carrozza, Venafro (CB) June 1986.

[28] Wanda Sellaci, San Giovanni Rotondo 7.12.1995.

[29] *Notes*...San Giovanni Rotondo, May 1993.

I continued in this way for several days until my next confession, when P. Pio said to me: "You've been moaning, filling the world with your lamentations".

"But Father, I haven't moaned about anything with anybody" I replied.

"Oh yes, really?", replied the Saint.

"I can assure you", I responded.

And he: "And who has been turning Heaven upside-down then?"[30]

2. Father Antonio Durante from Monterosso, a capuchin friar of the monastic province of Genoa and a missionary in Argentina, also had the chance to observe how once P. Pio read his thoughts.

Once on his return to Italy he received a permission from his superiors to go to San Giovanni Rotondo and stay for a while in that holy place. One day whilst walking with the Padre in front of the friary he noticed that Padre was the object of deferential affection and devotion from the people.

The good friar said to himself: "How can this man resist the temptation of vanity and of feeling pleased with himself".

He had not even finished conceiving this thought that the Saint turning towards him, smiling ,softly said to him: "Can you see how much glory of God?!".[31]

3. Father Pasquale Cattaneo has another testimony to give us about P. Pio's charismatic talents.

[30]   Margherita Cassano, San Giovanni Rotondo 6.9.1996.
[31]   Fr. Antonio Durante, born in Monterosso (GE) 7 August 1912 and died 11.June 1970 in La Plata, is described by his confreres as "a true son of St Francis, austere and good, uncompromising and affable". This testimony is given in Genoa by Fr. Riccardo Geminiani, capuchin friar, 20.4.1995.

He got off the train at Foggia station to catch the bus to San Giovanni Rotondo. As the bus went along the Puglia plain, he put to one side all the problems about which he would have spoken to the Padre and concentrated on a good examination of his conscience ready for confession.

With the help of the Holy Spirit he looked into every corner of his soul and made new proposals. However as the bus going to the Gargano was on the last part of the journey and the town came into view, he ended his examination perplexed thinking: "This spiritual life at times seems like trying to "climb glass"

When he arrived at the friary, he went into the sacristy and told the friar who helped with the confessions that he had come to confess and waited for his turn.

When he arrived, he entered the confessional, greeted P. Pio and made his confession. He talked about a few things on his mind and after receiving absolution and full answers to his problems, feeling happy he was about to leave, when the Padre looked at him amused and wittingly said: "So then, this spiritual life seems like climbing glass?"

Father Pasquale didn't say a word and was convinced that his spiritual Father was an enlightened man helped by the Holy Spirit to guide souls.[32]

A distinctive feature: the Padre can receive messages by telepathy

A very unusual truth is that P. Pio could perceive what his children were thinking, even without them speaking to him.

---

[32] Fr. Pasquale Cattaneo, Fiera di Primiero (TN) 31.7.1988.

1. Enzo Picciafuoco relates: "I had been told that to ask the Padre something in an effective way, it was necessary to do so during Mass, through thought. I tried it one day. But at the end of the Mass, after the Saint had given blessing, having the opportunity to speak to him I said: "Father, pray for my sister."

And he replied: "Haven't you already asked me?"

But this spiritual son had already realised this marvellous gift, since when P. Pio had begun to guide his spiritual life.

He confides to us: "The first night I spent at San Giovanni Rotondo I slept very little feeling emotional at the thought I was going to confess to the Padre. So I started to talk to his photos which were on the walls. I had a long chat.

The next day kneeling at his feet, I opened my heart to him and after receiving absolution I stayed in the sacristy to do penance.

But, when I saw that the saint, after ending confession, stayed sitting in his place, I went near him and asked if he could give me another five minutes. He answered: "You've been tormenting me last night, you carried on today and you still want another five minutes, do you?"

He got up and left to go back to the friary, but at the doorway he stopped and turning to me, said: "Act!"

He had understood my contemplative soul and was driving me to action".[33]

2. Lucietta Pennelli states:

"It was 25th May, the Padre's birthday. After Mass, as he went back to the sacristy, he passed near me and I in my mind said to the Lord: "Keep him safe for us for a long time".

A few days later, at the end of the confession, I said to him:

---

[33] Enzo Picciafuoco, Campobasso 22.7.1989.

"Happy Birthday Father, as on the 25th I wasn't able to give you my best wishes".

And P. Pio: "Haven't you already given me your best wishes?".[34]

3. A woman who had completely put herself into the Padre's hands to be led to God, states: "P. Pio was confessing the women and I was in the church at three or four metres from him. That day I wouldn't have had the chance to speak to him so I said to myself: "Father, send me a blessing. I need one".

I had just finished expressing my wish when I saw the Saint moving from the confessional window grate which hid his face, looking towards me and making the sign of the cross. Then he bowed his head once more to continue confessing."[35]

4. It was the second time that Teresa Venezia saw the Padre: after confession she waited in the cloister corridor to be able to kiss his hand as he passed by. When P. Pio arrived he didn't stop near her, he didn't put out his holy hand by which she wanted to be touched. She felt rather bad and lamented about this in her heart.

The Saint went back and like a father gruffly said: "Go on, kiss it, before I give you a smack on the face".[36]

5. Father Federico Carozza, our capuchin confrère tells us:
"A woman came to me, she was desperate, her husband had applied for a separation and had sent the documents to court

---

[34] Lucietta Pennelli 5.12.1995.
[35] Alma De Concini, Terzolas (TN) 23.7.1995.
[36] Teresa Venezia, Tolve (PZ) 19.10.1986.

through a lawyer; that day she would have learnt the results of the case. She needed to speak to P. Pio.

I told her: "Go in church, the Padre is praying on the balcony. Join your prayers to his and speak to him in your heart".

The woman did as the good friar had advised her.

When she returned to her hotel, she found a telephone message from her husband, begging her to return home where he was waiting to re-embrace her".[37]

"How many times you called me!"

However, it is to be noted that P. Pio listened to the voice of his spiritual children even when they were far from him.

1. Fr. Valentino from San Marco in Lamis, capuchin friar, during the second world war was in Emilia Romagna, whilst the Gothic line of the German Army, emplaced on the Apennines divided Italy in two. He hadn't heard from his family who lived in Puglia for a long time and decided one day to leave for the South.

However, it was necessary to cross the front and that was very risky.

As he knew some partisans who were fighting against the Germans, he asked them for help and advise about what to do. They indicated a way through the mountains. It was in the middle of the winter and it was dreadful weather. "It's tonight or never again" he said.

Together with others he set off walking. When they arrived high up there was a very narrow path covered with snow on a

---

[37]   Fr. Federico Carozza, Venafro June 1986.

steep slope. They took it. But when Fr. Valentino was halfway he put one foot wrong and started to slide.

" P. Pio help me, P. Pio help" cried the poor friar in anguish and terrified of falling.

He kept going down whilst calling for help to his spiritual father, when a bush broke his fall. The others helped him and he was able to continue his journey.

Once he crossed the line he was able to continue the journey home.

When he reached San Marco in Lamis, after resting a few hours, he wished to go to San Giovanni Rotondo to thank P. Pio who as soon as he saw him said: "How many times you called me that night, how many times!"

The Saint held him close to his heart and said: "Let us thank the Lord"[38]

"That night on the roofs!"

The testimony that follows is tragic-comic. But it is worth reading.

Father Nello Masini, a priest of the Giuseppini of San Leonardo Murialdo, met P. Pio in the 1950's and became one of his affectionate spiritual sons, thinking very highly of him. He often went down to San Giovanni Rotondo to stay a while with the Saint.

He tells us that during one Summer he went to Veneto to tale part with his confreres in a spiritual retreat.

He was quite chubby and well built and when he went to bed he snored extremely loudly. The brothers put him in an

---

[38] Fr. Valentino from San Marco in Lamis, San Severo (FG) 8.4.1992.

isolated room at the bottom of a long corridor far away from everyone so he wouldn't disturb anyone.

One night poor Father Nello, needing the bathroom went out of his room, and went into the nearby toilet, but closing the door too forcefully fastened the outer latch.

After satisfying his need, he wished to go out, but he realized he was trapped inside. He started to call for help but no one could hear him.

Losing all hope of being rescued, he climbed on a stool and looking out of the window saw the roof which was facing the rooms. He decided to try this way out, hoping he would find some window open.

He squeezed into the little space available to him but his 120 kilos were not of help and he got stuck halfway. His thoughts went to P. Pio whom he called upon many times.

Finally after many invocations he found himself outside on the roof top, without realizing how.

Holding onto the wall carefully, to avoid falling down into emptiness, he reached the windows. The first was closed but the second of the reading room was opened. He was finally able to reach his room.

The next morning he said to his brothers: "Good job that P. Pio helped me that night" and he told them of his adventure.

After a few months he returned once more to San Giovanni Rotondo to see and greet the Padre. He found him on the verandah praying.

He went towards him to kiss his hand. The Saint looked at him smiling and exclaimed: "Don Nello, Don Nello, that night on the roofs!"[39]

---

[39]   Carla Riceputi in Spronelli, the priest's niece, Cesena 29.11.2001

"Cordless" telephone

There is an important aspect to underline. P. Pio was able to establish an almost constant contact with the souls who turned to ask him questions from a distance in order to lead their spiritual lives.

When Eleonora Foresti had her first thought of finding an order of nuns, she came to San Giovanni Rotondo. To have his opinion. During her stay on the Gargano, she took the opportunity to confess to the Padre and have long chats concerning spiritual direction.

Getting used to an abundance of spiritual light and comfort before leaving to return home, she made Nina Campanile, who at the time was very close to her, promise she would keep in touch with the Padre. Between the two an epistolary correspondence was established in which Foresti asked questions and Campanile gave P. Pio's answers.

Once Eleonora wrote to her: "Tell the Padre it is not enough that his answers come by letter. I need to feel him spiritually".

Nina told this to the Saint who answered: "All right, we will use telepathy".

After a while Campanile received a letter from Foresti which said: "Tell the Padre that the "cordless" telephone works extremely well".[40]

---

[40] Testimony by Nina Campanile, registered on tape in San Giovanni Rotondo by Fr Gerardo Saldutto on 1.9.1973. About Foresti see "The Padre I", p.33.

2. Clairvoyance

The capacity to sum up a situation and foresee future developments can be attributed to shrewdness or intuition; but mystic experience shows us that often the Saints see certain situations and their evolution by means which are not natural but are revaluations from God.

This happened frequently in P. Pio's lifetime with regards to the past, present or future events.

1. I accompanied the Padre to the sacristy one morning for Holy Mass. It was early and the Holy Brother asked me: "Has Father Giuseppe come yet?". I answered that the sacristan still hadn't opened the church.

The Padre meanwhile dressed in holy vestments, and hearing the noise of people taking their places in church, repeated the question. I went into the church and asked if amongst the priests there was one called Father Giuseppe. Nobody came forwards.

I told all this to the Padre, who after a few minutes asked me again: "Has Father Giuseppe come?"

This time I was luckier and took the priest into the sacristy. As soon as he entered, the Padre turned to him and nodded to him to come nearer; he hugged him and he went towards the altar.

After Mass Fr Giuseppe said he was surprised that the Saint had been looking for him; nobody could have told the Padre about his arrival as he hadn't spoken to anybody about this trip. I was not surprised: we friars were used to such things.

Father Giuseppe whilst giving me Christmas wishes in December 1996, reminded me of the episode and thanked me for "the special favour he had received through me", but in truth I did nothing for him.[41]

---

[41] Don Giuseppe Villa from S. Angelo Taizzano (TR).

It could surprise one that the Padre could show this charism even in everyday simple things but it often happened.

2. One day Rosa Albina Valente brought a very nice apple from Rodi Garganico (FG) and gave it to Father Vincenzo from Montemarano, asking him to personally deliver it to P. Pio.

At midday, the porter carrying out her wish, went up to the Padre who was sitting at his place in the refectory and put the apple on the table. The Padre looked at it and said: "This comes from Rodi!"

That good soul of Father Vincenzo laughing said he was right and was not at all surprised by the Saint's declaration.[42]

3. Giuseppe Cassano from San Giovanni Rotondo had arranged the date of his wedding and went up to the friary to inform P. Pio. "Father, I'm getting married on 12 September, Our Lady's name day".

"No" said the Saint, "You will get married on 8 September, Our Lady's birthday."

The young man was very surprised by what the Padre said but made no comment.

He went back home and met his mother who said: Listen, your cousin has decided to get married on 12 September, and as the guests are more or less those we have invited to your wedding it would be better to change the date. I think September 8th is a good alternative.

Giuseppe said nothing, P. Pio had already given him this date.[43]

---

[42] Rosa Albina Valente, 7.4.1987.
[43] Iole Cassano, San Giovanni Rotondo 26.11.2005.

4. Dr Angelo Ruzzi, a doctor from Tolve (Pz) much amused tells us about his first meeting with P. Pio.

We went to San Giovanni Rotondo at the end of the 30s' and stayed there a few days. In those times one could really enjoy the Padre's company as the pilgrims were allowed into the garden and could sometimes stop and chat with the Saint.

The day after his arrival the doctor was in the garden with another visitor to whom he presented himself saying: "I'm Angelo Ruzzi".

The other visitor did not understand and asked: "I beg your pardon?"

At that moment P. Pio arrived and said to the doctor: "Go on and say that you are don Raffaele or this fellow won't know who you are".

Raffaele was the second name of Dr. Ruzzi and at Tolve, where he was a doctor, he was known with the addition of the title "don", a courtesy title given in the south of Italy not only to priests but also to doctors.[44]

5. The father of a spiritual daughter from Modena came to San Giovanni Rotondo for the first time, he went to the friary to greet the Padre, who as soon as he saw him said: "You are Adriana's father aren't you?"[45]

6 When Assunta Massa had her first son, she wished to give him the name of his grandfather Francesco, but all the family started to call him Franco.

The day of the baptism they took the little boy to the friary where they waited for P. Pio who was to baptise the child. They said to the Saint that the boy would be called Francesco.

[44]   Angelo Ruzzi, Tolve (Pz) 18.10.1986.
[45]   Adriana Pallotti, San Giovanni Rotondo, 5.12.1995.

The Padre, after pouring water on the baptized baby's head stroking his head with his half-closed hand said: "Little beautiful Franco, Francolino so beautiful![46]

We must say that sometimes P. Pio gave the impression that he played with his charisms, because it was so natural to him.

Some excellent Swiss cheese had been given to E. M. and she quickly decided to give some to P. Pio, because when she saw spiritual daughters who had enough means to give presents to the Padre she was rather envious.

She was poor and what she could gain from her job she gave monthly to the Saint for "The Home for the Relief of Suffering".

She gave the little parcel to Pietro Cugino, who was often by P. Pio's side, praying him to give it to P. Pio as soon as possible. The good blind fellow promised he would do so that very night.

But when he went to the Padre's side to accompany him back to his room the Saint said: "Give me what you have otherwise that woman will start crying: "I'm poor, I'm poor![47]

This joking tone was used by P. Pio also for things that were much more important, for example, binding himself for life to a son, undergoing a strong spiritual crisis because of his father's illness.

It happened to Piero Melillo, when he came for the first time to San Giovanni Rotondo in 1955. The meeting began with an ironic joking remark.

---

[46] Assunta Massa, San Giovanni Rotondo 29.01.2005, day on which Francesco celebrated his 25th wedding anniversary in the shrine of Our Lady of Grace.

[47] Notes…San Giovanni Rotondo May 1993.

"One summer evening in that year, Piero received a visit in his study from a dear friend of his who was a doctor like him, who had left Milan and moved to San Giovanni Rotondo to organize, with other colleagues, the opening of the hospital "The Home for the Relief of Suffering". And he spoke to him of P. Pio.

The news about the Saint has little interest for Piero, but after a few months his father suddenly became seriously ill. Facing this drama of his loved one, the doctor felt he was alone and impotent against this impossible situation.

His thought flew to the Padre. He decided to go down to the South of Italy to meet him. Arriving at San Giovanni Rotondo, he met his colleague who told him he wanted to introduce him to the Saint.

It was a very hot August day: when they arrived in the friary, the two went towards the terrace where they found P. Pio breathing a little fresh air cooled by the evening breeze and enjoying a few moment's rest surrounded by confrères and friends.

Piero knelt down to kiss the Padre's hand and on rising caught the Saint's glance who scrutinizing him said "Where are you from?"

The doctor with a touch of pride replied: "From Milan!"

The Saint looked at him again and added ironically: "Oh, *oriundo*! Tomorrow you will tell me why you have come here!"

Melillo was amazed: he had almost forgotten he had been born in Trani, in Puglia: he had only spent the first ten days of his life there.

The word "*oriundo*" meaning a citizen of "foreign extraction" which P. Pio certainly couldn't have read on his birth certificate, gave Piero a clear indication about what was said about the Saint's charism.

The next day in the afternoon, he went to confess to P. Pio and spoke about his fathers' illness.

From that day the Padre kept Piero near him, so much that Piero, as well as operating each month in P. Pio's hospital without being paid, established his family's summer home in San Giovanni Rotondo.[48]

The Padre reassures and tranquillizes

Carlo Colalillo states: "Long ago on 1st August 1946, I was discharged from the army where I had been the veterinary Officer. I was impatient to finally return home where my elderly parents, my wife of a few years, and my little daughter Nicla, who I had seen only once, were all waiting for me.

After my initial joy at returning home, I started to worry about my insertion into civil life and new job. I didn't wish to be a burden to my father especially as I had a new family.

Of course I spoke about my worries to my parents and one day I opened my heart to my sister Alfonsina, who was leaving for San Giovanni Rotondo to confess to P. Pio: she assured me she would have spoken about my problem to him and that she would have asked him to pray for me.

P. Pio reassured her immediately, saying that I had already been sorted out. As she couldn't quite understand what the Saint was telling her, she thought the good Padre just wanted to consol her and continued to ask for his help.

So the Padre said to her: "Have you or have you not understood that your brother already has a job?" At this point

---

[48] From a written testimony by Piero Melillo..

my sister remained silent even though she continued not to understand.

That same evening she returned home: she told me of her conversation with P. Pio and that the holy Friar had amongst other things assured her that I would never again have to worry about my future.

It is easy to imagine how astonished Alfonsina was when I told her that at her departure I had been nominated for an important veterinary position which was available because the previous vet had moved to Northern Italy.

Is this not one of the miracles of our loved P. Pio?[49]

A son who trusted the Padre

Many spiritual children enjoyed the charisms with which P. Pio had been enriched from Heaven.

Enzo Picciafuoco, from Ancona was engaged to Emilia Barone from Campobasso. Before taking that step as a good spiritual son who did nothing without seeking the Padre's opinion he asked if his choice of future bride was a good one P. Pio answered: "I believe so".

Once being at San Giovanni Rotondo, he thought that on his way back home, he could have stopped in Molise to call in and see his girlfriend. Naturally he spoke to P. Pio to see what he thought. The Saint answered with much nonchalance: "If they don't throw you out!"

Enzo wasn't very satisfied with this answer which he couldn't understand as his relationship with the girl's family

---

[49] Testimony written by Dr. Carlo Colalillo 7 October 1986. Boiano (CB).

was very good. He begged Fr. Innocenzo, his friend, to ask the Padre what he meant, but the latter without adding any further explanations said: "I have told him what I had to say".

The young man took the train but decided to go straight home without stopping off at Campobasso as P. Pio hadn't given his full approval.

When he arrived at Ancona, he found an express letter from Emilia, saying that if he was thinking of going to visit her it was better to put it off until another moment as her house was like a military hospital, everyone was ill except for her and she was being their nurse.

Enzo confirmed his belief that trusting in the Padre was to choose with his help whatever was best. He saw this in a situation in which there could have been a death in his family.

The young couple did get married and they had a large family. When his wife Emilia was expecting her sixth child, Enzo, as he had done for the previous pregnancies, decided to go to San Giovanni Rotondo to speak to the Padre who had always calmed and reassured him that all would go well. He came down from Ancona and said to the Saint: "Father, as always just the midwife?"

And P. Pio both worried and serious replied: "Doctors will be needed, you'll need doctors!"

Enzo returned home very worried and agitated. Emilia was taken to hospital, where she was immediately operated: the baby was dead and she was in serious danger. After two days a friend of the family went to San Giovanni Rotondo and asked P. Pio to pray for Emilia. He replied: "I'll pray that all ends well".

The friend returned to Ancona and told those involved what P. Pio had said. Emilia listened to the Saint's words and said to herself: "The Padre doesn't know that all has ended…badly".

But the day after whist she was in bed being visited by a friend, she had a violent haemorrhage. Later she confessed: "I felt as if my blood was abandoning me, my vision became blurred and I passed out".

Her friend quickly called for help and the patient was saved.

When Emilia remembers that tragic moment, she says: "If I had been on my own I would have bled to death in a few minutes. This time too the Padre had seen clearly, right to the end.[50]

Uncertainties highly paid for

Not always those who had received advice were ready to make the most of it.

Giuseppe Barbagallo from Catania went to San Giovanni Rotondo in May 1968 to confess to P. Pio. After he received absolution he said: "Father, I've met a girl and I'd like to marry her".

And the Saint replied: "Have you told her, have you asked her yet?"

"No, Father" replied the young man.

"Well, what are you waiting for, that she comes to you, if she has no idea of your intentions?"

Giuseppe returned home but because he was feeling so shy he wasted time instead of declaring his feelings. In August of the same year, a month before, P. Pio died he returned once more to San Giovanni and confessed; then he said to the Saint: "Father, I still haven't talked to that girl".

---

[50] Enzo Picciafuoco, Campobasso 23.7.1989.

"And what can you say to her now!?" replied the Padre. Then turning towards him, but with a gaze that went far away, the Saint started to speak an unknown language that was neither modern nor classical. At the end he said: "Persist and you will receive help.".

Of course the young man understood nothing of this mysterious language, but he asked: "Why haven't I got to say anything to that girl?" His doubts ended when he returned to Catania and learnt that she had got engaged to someone else.

Later on he met a girl he married who bore him two children, Francesco and Chiara. When these were little, she was struck with multiple sclerosis and had to use a wheelchair.

In those moments of much sufferance and unhappiness, the bond between Giuseppe and P. Pio who had already gone to Heaven, became even stronger. And invoking him often and being aware of his protection and assistance Giuseppe realised what the Saint's last world to him had been: "Persist and you will be helped".

Those words became his viaticum in the difficult way ahead.[51]

"Those poor people"

Adriana Pallotti is one of those spiritual daughters who left their home towns to move and settle in San Giovanni Rotondo in order to be near the Padre. She too before making any decision asked him for advise. One day she asked: "Father, is it a good idea to go and visit my relatives?".

---

[51]   Giuseppe Barbagallo, Giarre (CT) 25.04.1998.

"Yes, do go and visit those poor people!", answered the Saint.

Adriana was rather surprised by the Padre's answer. She left for Modena and when she arrived home found her family suffering with TBC, and some where in a serious condition. She stayed a long time with them and was convinced even more that her spiritual father was God's servant and illuminated by Him. [52]

Let us add another testimony.

1. Giovanna Russo: "One day whilst I was getting ready to go to Mass, my mother had pains in her heart, they were so strong she feared the end was at hand. I wanted to stay at home, but my mum insisted: "Go to the Friary, go to the Padre and tell him to pray for me".

I obeyed. Once inside the church I went to the confessional. I had received permission to enter, but all I could do was cry. At last the Padre managed to let me speak. Then he said, almost casually, as if it wasn't important: "You always see the dark side! She's alright and perhaps she's chatting with the neighbours".

P. Pio continued confessing and I moved away; I sat on a church bench but I couldn't calm down.

Fr. Luciano De Paola from Capracotta, who checked the order of the confessions, who had heard what the Padre had told me, on seeing that I was still crying, came near and said: "Don't you trust the Padre's words? Shall we bet that your mother is fine now?".

After saying this Fr Luciano offered to take me home. When I went in, I saw mum chatting with her friends".[53]

---

[52]   Adriana Pallotti, San Giovanni Rotondo 05.12. 1995.
[53]   Giovanna Russo, San Giovanni Rotondo 2.12.1985.

2. Iole Cassano recounts.

"Between 1933 and 1934 there was an epidemic of scarlet fever in San Giovanni Rotondo which caused many deaths. I was quite young when I became ill.

One morning my dad, seeing I had a high temperature and fearing the worst went to the friary to speak to P. Pio.

The Padre listened carefully and then smiling said to him, "Don't worry, go home and you'll see the girl no longer has a high temperature!"

And it was true.[54]

3. Vincenzo Saponaro, a teacher at a state infant junior school, lived at Tolve, a little town in the province of Potenza. Thinking of his children's future studies, he had settled in Naples after asking for and obtaining a transfer. As time passed by, he began to have some serious doubts about his decision and asked Dr. Giovanni Delfino, a well thought of spiritual son of the Padre, to accompany him to San Giovanni Rotondo to ask P. Pio's advice as to what he should do.

When the two arrived at the friary, Giovanni who knew P. Pio's ways very well, said to his friend who was waiting with others in the corridor for the Padre to pass by : "If the Holy man stops in front of you, that means he will speak to you". And the Saint stopped.

"Father", said Vincenzo, "I have moved to Naples. I don't know whether I should move back to my home town of Tolve". P. Pio replied: "Go back home my sons, go back home".

Dr. Delfino interrupted saying: "But Father, he has three sons who after Junior School must continue their studies".

The Padre replied: "But there are schools everywhere!". It

---

[54] Iole Cassano San Giovanni Rotondo 26.11.2004.

was in 1960 and at Tolve there were no secondary-schools; however Vincenzo Saponaro followed P. Pio's advice. After a short time even in that little town a secondary-school was built.[55]

3. P. Pio reveals the plan that God has for souls

1. A girl was strongly attracted to religious life but was tied by a family situation that did not allow her to make her wish become reality. One day she went up to San Giovanni Rotondo to ask P. Pio for advice about her doubts. As soon as she entered the confessional, before she said a word, the Padre opened the grate and started to speak; but she didn't understand a word.

She asked the Saint for an explanation and he raising his voice said: "Do you understand you have a vocation, do you understand you have a vocation?"

The young girl, very embarrassed, told him that as her parents were dead and she was the eldest sister she felt responsible for her brothers.

P. Pio replied: "And what are you going to be, a servant for your brothers all your life?"

The girl wanted to say something, and when the Padre said in a peremptory tone that which Jesus said to those called to follow him who put obstacles in the way: *"Leave the dead to bury their dead"* (Luke 9,60)

She was very much upset by this and was ready to leave the confessional, but the Padre called her back: "Come here, I have to give you absolution". At the end of the confession, the girl almost ran away to catch the bus which would take her

---

[55]   Vincenzo Saponaro, San Giovanni Rotondo 17.12.1996.

home; but on the threshold of the church a mysterious force pushed her backwards. She felt obliged to retrace her steps, and in doing so she caught the gentle gaze of P. Pio.

She did her penance and together with a feeling of great peace, she could smell a perfume which stayed with her until she left.

The woman who gave us this testimony added: "I am a nun thanks to him".[56]

2. Sister Mansueta Loconte, a Clarisse in the monastery of S. Quirico di Assisi talks about her meeting with P. Pio.

"In March 1947, I, Antonietta Laconte, together with my father Ignazio and my deaf and dumb sister Pasqua, went on a pilgrimage to San Giovanni Rotondo to have a talk with P. Pio. There were various reasons which had pushed us to make this trip from our town, Fasano near Brindisi, to the Gargano; especially considering our financial situation which was in difficulty at the end of the war.

My father, most of all, wanted to beseech the Lord's grace for my deaf and dumb sister. I, who also shared this intention, wished to have my idea of becoming a nun, which had been in my heart for a while, confirmed.

The day after our arrival, my father hurried to the sacristy, also because he had to personally deliver a letter from our friend Palmina Guarini, who wished to enter the Poor Clare's monastery of S. Quirico di Assisi. He managed to speak to the Padre, who after a while went to the woman's confessional.

When my turn arrived, I knelt down and immediately began to speak of my calling to become a nun, but also the worries I

---

[56]   Sr Giulia Schettini, Cassano Murge (BA) 27.4.1992.

had thinking about leaving my father on his own with my deaf and dumb sister, especially as my mother had died 31 March 1933.

P. Pio confirmed I had a vocation and said to me: "Be sure that the Lord will call you to monastic life". But to my great surprise the Padre added that I wouldn't have been able to carry out the Lord's plans for me, if I didn't fight against my capital vice: pride! The Padre was right; in fact, for me, only what I did or thought was right!

I was struck and astounded by another thing. P. Pio told me to tell my friend, Palmina Guarini he would answer her letter with a prayer. How could he have known that I was the daughter of that gentleman who a little while before had given him Palmina's letter? And then he hadn't had the time to read that letter!

Once back home I had quite an inner struggle to accept what with gentleness the Padre had shown me my true problem: pride and obstinacy.

With the Lord's help and the strength that P. Pio's words gave me, I was able to carry out my vocation to the contemplative life in an enclosed order, together with my friend Palmina Guarini, known as sister Chiara Rosati. We have been in the same monastery in Assisi for 50 years.

We entered the monastery in the same year on 24th September 1947.[57]

3. Following now is a declaration written by sister Chiara Rosaria Guarini, the nun mentioned in the former testimony.

"How P. Pio saved my vocation to be a Poor Clare".

I was just seventeen when I felt the first inclination of a vo-

---

[57]   Testimony written by Sr. Mansueta Loconte, Assisi 5.9.1996.

cation. I was a carefree girl who enjoyed life with little knowledge of spiritual values.

I spoke to a priest by chance and managed to make a few steps in the darkness. I felt that my soul was invaded by God's presence but I found it extremely difficult to come to terms with myself and realise what was happening to me. I realised that by myself I couldn't manage, and it was then that providence helped me through a holy priest who could clearly see my intentions, and for a good seven years guided me to realise a true calling to a holy life of contemplation.

I contacted the Poor Clares of Assisi and after many letters they said they trusted me to be suitable to have a trial run in their monastery.

I had to face some obstacles. I was the only support my fifty year old widowed mother had. My two elder brothers were serving in the army during World War II. The younger was a P.O.W. in Scotland. I was pushed into making a pact with the Lord. I would leave my mother, if my two brothers came home safe and sound.

And so it was that during 1945-46 both happily returned home. Mother was prepared to do all to carry out God's will, but my elder brother and my uncle who had acted as head of the house put obstacles in my way, it was a hard battle but I managed to overcome even this.

When all seemed settled I was stormed with uncertainties and doubts about my calling which seemed presumptuous and not at all inspired by God. I broke off with my spiritual director.

One day I was ill in bed with a high temperature and by chance a friend, Antonietta Loconte called telling me she was going to see P. Pio, the capuchin Friar of San Giovanni Rotondo. The idea of giving her my letter came to mind, after she promised me she would personally give it to the Saint.

When my friend arrived at P. Pio's friary, she was surprised by the large crowd around the confessional, and thought it best to give my letter to her father, because the men had the privilege of confessing in the sacristy, face to face with the confessor. The letter arrived to P. Pio and he put it in his pocket.

The Saint then went to confess the women in the church confessional; even though she was in the midst of a large crowd, my friend's turn arrived and before she said anything he pulled the letter from his pocket saying: "Tell the person who has written to me that I will answer by prayer".

After a month on exactly 30th April 1947 I went to San Giovanni Rotondo with the intention of meeting P. Pio. I went into the Church whilst they were uncovering the picture of our lady of Grace, for the beginning of her holy month of May. I took it as a good sign.

In the middle of a large and noisy crowd, my turn finally arrived. I started with a few words: "Father, it seemed as if I had a vocation for the contemplative life; I've tried to nourish it but at the end of seven years, I feel I've been misleading myself. I ask you if I'm mistaken".

And he answered: "Certainly!"

I continued: "Is mine a true vocation?"

And he said: "Certainly!"

"Perhaps I should try again?"

And he for the third time: "Certainly!" He ended speaking at the top of his voice: "Be careful, the Lord can punish you"

I went home feeling recharged ready to throw myself in the arms of He who was calling me. I decided to change route and carry out my plan for total adhesion to his following.

I faced all, and then together with my mother arranged my entrance into the monastery for the first week of October.

At the beginning of September I returned to San Giovanni

Rotondo with the intention of asking P. Pio for his blessing and confessing to him once more.

With difficulty going through an exuberant crowd I finally reached the confessional. I started speaking with no reference to my previous confession in May. I did it on purpose with the intention of being recognized without presenting myself.

"Father, I have come to ask you for your blessing before I enter the nunnery".

He, without asking for any explanation, with the air of one who already knew all, answered in a strong jubilant voice: "My fullest blessings, my fullest blessings!"

Then calmly, nearly speaking with monosyllables, he pronounced other words I couldn't make out; I just caught the word "prophecy".

The following October 11th entered the monastery; that day's liturgy celebrated the maternity of Our Blessed Lady: this too I considered a good sign. I walked under the gaze of Our Lady, until I professed my solemn vows on 21st May 1952. It took great determination!

Uncertainty and fear were the two borders that characterized my ways towards Christ. Later all finally changed: I discovered love and this freed me.

On May 11th 1999, if the Lord lets me live so long I will celebrate 50 years profession, with a heart filled to the brim of experience of the great wonders he, in his infinite mercy, has carried out within me, as in no one else…I am full of enthusiasm and overflowing with joy!"[58]

---

[58]   Testimony written by Sister Chiara Rosaria Guaria, Assisi 5.9.1996.

4. The Spirit of prophecy

St Paul speaks of this gift in both the letter to the Corinthians and to the Romans. Prophecy here means the capability or power to speak under the influence of the Holy Spirit for the improvement of the community. The peculiarity of charism is to receive a message from God, the oracle, to communicate to definite addresses: the members of God's people.

Regarding the gifts with which the Holy spirit assists the Church, it has been written that: "the most important charisms are those that build most, that is those that have a very evident missionary destination". The gift of prophecy is to be found in this dimension.[59]

The Lord's prophet, is a name fitting to P. Pio; he widely spread God's word. Not by going from town to town as Jesus did, to whose image he remained faithful, but by staying shut away in a remote friary.

There wasn't even a decent road, when the Saint began his apostolic work, but still many ran to his call. Day by day God's spirit led them near to him so that he could speak to them in God's name.

As a prophet the Padre was true to his calling, speaking God's truth without compromise, constantly without fail, with the same pugnacious spirit which made him similar to the ancient prophets.

This has already been said and now we wish to point out some other particulars.

---

[59]   NUOVO DIZIONARIO DI SPIRITUALITÀ by Stefano De Fiores and Tullio Goffi. Ed Paoline, 1979, 166.

a) Training

Not every one can teach a subject or a skill, you need a good teacher; even transmitting facts or doctrine is not easy; they say you need a special gift to do so; but teaching the way to regulate oneself in the spiritual field, is only possible to who-ever is enlightened by God.

P. Pio led souls in a specific way, teaching and training, in two precise moments of his life: when he formed his first groups of spiritual daughters through weekly conferences, as soon as he arrived in San Giovanni Rotondo in 1916, and when secluded and thoughtful in his cell, for several years, up to 1923, he sent his precious writings to souls thirsty for God's words.[60]

It seems that the Padre missed teaching the catechism. The following episode illustrates this.

In 1965 Father Michele Farulli, parish priest in San Severo (FG) went with the Bishop of Ostuni Cathedral, Mons Aleo who was a famous catechist, to San Giovanni Rotondo. Whilst presenting him to the Padre, his intense activity in the field of teaching God's word was underlined.

P. Pio listened attentively and then exclaimed: "If only I had always done catechism!"

Mgr. Aleo was deeply affected by P. Pio's words and con-fessed that at a certain point of his apostolic work, putting to one side the spreading of God's truth by word of mouth, he thought it a good idea to make use of the cinema as an educa-tive tool for catechism. It was a complete failure in all ways: especially economically as it made large loss.[61]

---

[60]   See p. 458.
[61]   Fr Michele Farulli, San Severo (FG), 2.2.1986.

The Padre however carried out teachings, whilst giving the sacrament of penance or in short private chats. He only had a little time and so the Holy Spirit's help was absolutely necessary.

The Padre's teachings, contained in a few words, were always personalized. To souls who found themselves in the same conditions and circumstances, he offered different suggestions.

We have a symbolic example of this in what Mariangela Casu from Oristano tells us. She was at San Giovanni Rotondo for years under P. Pio's spiritual guide.

She had a friend, Anna Banni, who was a baby-sitter for a family with a lot of small children, and so she didn't sleep a lot at night. One day this girl complained to P. Pio: "Sometimes during your Mass I fall asleep. It's better that I don't come."

"No my daughter, you must come because you meet Jesus", he answered, "when you feel you are falling asleep, don't worry. The apostles did the same in the garden of olives didn't they? Just make sure you are near the column so people don't see you nodding off".

Anna obeyed her spiritual father.

Mariangela, hearing what the Saint had said to her friend and having the same difficulty, in a confession said: "Father, I sometimes fall asleep in your Mass". She waited for an understanding word.

But P. Pio was severe and demanding. "Well then, stand up, because you fall asleep when you are kneeling down!"[62]

The Padre taught like this with little touches of wisdom.

1. A spiritual daughter tell us: "One day P. Pio made me

---

[62]   Mariangela Casu, Oristano 21.4.1999.

understand how I should position myself in adoration in front of Jesus during communion.

I went to the little friary church to take part in the Padre's Mass. When the rosary was over I lent my folding chair to another woman and I knelt down. However as I felt cold because it was the middle of winter, I folded my scarf over a couple of times to make a cushion which I knelt upon.

A few days later, I went to confession and heard the Saint reprove me, though I had said nothing: "I will teach you to put rags under your knees when you are in front of Jesus in the Blessed Sacrament."[63]

2 In November 1958 Dr. Pietro Melillo and the architect Geppino Gentile, who was following the work on the new church which was being built at San Giovanni Rotondo found themselves in P. Pio's cell with other confreres of the Saint. It was evening and those present lingered a while with the Padre hoping he would take a well earned rest, when the architect said he had dreamt some lucky numbers.

The doctor, he himself admits, was a gambler like his grandfather and father before him, especially for the lottery. Thinking he might be onto a good thing he encouraged the architect to tell him the numbers he planned to play.

His friend wasted no time and started to give him the numbers. At the first number P. Pio remained silent, but with little nods of his head agreed; at the second number he touched the doctor's arm with his elbow to catch his attention and he corrected one of the numbers; for the third and fourth number he showed complete indifference.

The doctor, on his return to Milan went to the lottery of-

63   E. Mori, San Giovanni Rotondo, 30.9.1994.

fice and bet on the set of four numbers, but before leaving he became doubtful, thinking of the Padre's behaviour whilst the architect rattled off the numbers. So he played an "ambo" (two numbers). The following Saturday the "ambo" came up but not the four numbers. He won 25.000 Lira.

When he returned again to San Giovanni Rotondo he gave half of the money to P. Pio; but on doing so he regretted the fact that the other numbers hadn't been correct. If they had he would have been able to set himself up as he was at the beginning of his profession.

The Padre thanked him for his gift which would go towards the hospital and looking at him in a fatherly stern tome said: "What I did was only to teach you that gambling is not for you!"

From that day onwards the doctor gambled no more.[64]

3. Eligio D'Antonio narrates that, whilst P. Pio was greeting some Swiss people in the corridor on the first floor of the friary, one of them said: "Father, how beautiful you are!". "Thanks for the compliment", said the Padre, "At last there is someone who says I am beautiful! And yet many run off when they see me!".

But soon after, even then he wished to give guidance, he added: "With regards to beauty I have said many times, those who wish to live well and into old age should first prepare their old age and then their youth".

Some of those present did not understand his meaning and so he explained that "in youth one shouldn't exasperate oneself with vices if they want a good old age".[65]

---

[64] Testimony written by Piero Melillo.
[65] Testimony written by Wanda Sellach.

When the Padre had to make use of doctrine he did so in simple clear language.

Prof. Michele Melillo, a well cultured man who had a good relationship with P. Pio thanks to periodic spiritual conversations, possible because he lived nearby in Siponto (Manfredonia) one day said to the Saint: "Father, tell me something that will be useful to live by all my life!"

And P. Pio synthetized everything in an expression from the old catechism: "Remember that you have been born "to know, to love and serve God, to be happy with him eternally in Heaven".[66]

It must be noted that the effectiveness and invaluable use of this method was not always appreciated.

One day Fr. Teofilo dal Pozzo, the provincial minister of Foggia, who came from Tuscany asked Pietro Cugino to go with him to visit Elena Bandini[67], who was also from Tuscany.

He wished to ask her advice as she had a saintly disposition.

As the two walked along linking each other, the priest said he was worried about problems in the province and the difficulties he was having with things that were not going well. The poor blind Pietro listened, but at a pause in the conversation said: "Listen Father, I am very sorry…People from all over the world come to San Giovanni to ask P. Pio for advice and they are all satisfied. You have a light and you are not making use of it". The invitation to turn to the Padre, to shed light on how

---

[66] Michele Melillo, San Giovanni Rotondo, March 1994.

[67] Elena Bandini, born in Borgo San Lorenzo, (FI). She died in San Giovanni Rotondo 25 October 1955. In 1937 she settled in San Giovanni Rotondo, near P. Pio with whom she had been exchanging letters since 1921.

to govern the religious province was clear.

Fr Teofilo replied: "Yes, Pietro, but many times P. Pio gives advice which seems to come from an infant school".

Pietro Cugino, a simple man, attentive to every word from the Padre, notes that the tendency to teach was so born in P. Pio "that even when in a moment of relaxation he told jokes, he always added a moral touch".[68]

b) Exhortation

Encouraging people to be virtuous was a continuous task for P. Pio; and if the confessional was the place where he preferred to do this, he didn't miss the opportunity to remind people of their duty to be "good Christians", even day trippers.

We know that when the Padre returned to his room after confessions, he could meet not only individuals, but also little groups who waited as he passed by the friary or sacristy. He didn't miss giving them his message which was short but rich in context.

Diligent Fr Costantino Capobianco from Fragneto Manforte (BN) capuchin friar who drew up the Chronicle of the friary of San Giovanni Rotondo, from the notes the brother friars who lived near the Saint gave him, shows us a Padre who was always ready to take each opportunity to exhort and remind one of their duty.

"30 April 1954.

The secretary of the Communist party of Sesto Fiorentino, one Gino Targioni, has been to see P. Pio who called him by

---

[68]   Pietro Cugino, San Giovanni Rotondo, May 1993.

name although he had never met him before, and he told him: "You must put one hand one your forehead and the other one on your heart. Remember we must see each other more than once. You must not close your ears to God's voice which is following you!"" (f. 356).

"22 June 1954.

Amongst the numerous pilgrims, there are a lot of Carabinieri (policemen), whom the Padre has encouraged to do their duty for their Country in God's name". (f. 371)

"17 April 1955.

P. Pio received and blessed the theological and philosophical Study of the Franciscans of Benevento with the encouraging words "to be sons of St Francis in the true sense of real Friars Minor". (f. 399)

"18-20 April 1955.

A very busy day, there were a lot of foreign priests, German, Belgium and Brazilian. They came to the Padre to be blessed and assisted in their ministry. P. Pio blessed them all and explained: "All you faithful soldiers! Let's die on the breach!"" (f. 388).

"23 April 1955.

Young people from the Jesuit College of Naples were here to be blessed by P. Pio who said to them: "Along with the traditional work for human science, which your Company feels is important don't forget to hold onto the need for pity. More pity than science! Only prayers save souls"" (f. 400).

"23 April 1955.

The lawyers from Cerignola came to see P. Pio and he whilst blessing them reminded them of their Christian duty whist carrying out their profession". (f. 400).

"12 may 1955.

We noticed students from various colleges, governed by Jesuits, Brothers of Christian Schools and Salesians, who have invaded the friary. "Young men, study", said P. Pio, "but most of all pray! Prayer alone can save souls"" (f. 403).

"4 June 1955.

The general Visitor of the Friars Minor of the Province of Foggia came with a group of students from the nearby friary of San Matteo. The Padre stayed with them cheerfully and blessed them all putting his hand on their heads and saying: "Let us make St Francis proud of us""(f. 106).

"8-12 June 1955.

A lot of priests came in these days. The Padre blessed them all inciting them to prayer, "the only way to save the world"" (f. 406).

"10 August 1955.

Towards evening, in the little room on the first floor, just after the stairs, Giovanni Leone, M.P. president of the Chamber of Deputies, together with some members of his party waited for P. Pio. They spent almost half an hour with him, speaking of Italy and firmly indicating the way to insist upon in politics: that permeated by Christian spirit.

He gave a bitter judgment of the way the nation had been governed in the past, especially their compromising attitude with the opposition: "If I told you that you were co-operators or indirectly collaborators, would I be mistaken?".

The honourable M.P. was rather surprised, but the Padre instead of sweetening his tone continued his reprimand"(f. 410).

"25-27 August 1955.

There are many Italian and foreign priests.

P. Pio blessed them all inciting them to do their apostolic work faithfully" (f. 412).

"16 June 1957.

As he walked in the cloisters after the evening service some nuns asked him for a spiritual thought for the week. He answered: "We are in Corpus Domini week...Give yourselves generously to Jesus without holding back, as he gave himself to us completely"" (f. 449).

"8 September 1957.

A large group of artillerymen stationed at Foggia with their colonel and various officials, came to see P. Pio, who received them in the lane opposite the refectory windows. The colonel spoke for all: "Father bless us all. And P. Pio: "I bless you all and hope the nation will not need you".

The colonel's eyes were damp with emotion, but he was taken aback by the Padre's words; the Padre continued: "I spoke well, because when the nation does not need you, it means we are at peace" (f. 452-453).

One more comment on this subject:

One day Fr. Domenico Serini and some youths who attended the "*Centro Formazione Professionale*" (Professional Training Institute) of San Giovanni Rotondo went to see P. Pio who spoke to the boys with fatherly goodness saying: "Learn a trade, but most of all be good Christians".[69]

c) Advice

Part of the prophecy of charism is to keep people on the straight and narrow road. The Saint's words and advice were specific and adapted to each particular situation and person whether they asked him for his opinion or not. The following testimony is an example of this.

Dr Angelo Raffaele Ruzzi who met P. Pio at the end of the 1930's at the outbreak of World War II was recalled to the army as medical lieutenant. After some temporary posts he was assigned to Manfredonia to his great joy because he could easily go up to San Giovanni Rotondo to greet, speak and confess to him.

During one of his visits, he went into the sacristy whilst waiting for the Saint. When P. Pio arrived a young soldier who was next to him asked: "Father, I've been engaged for a few years and I'd like to get married".

The Saint answered: "What do you mean you want to get married whilst the war in on? What if you have a child and they send you to the front, how could you live knowing you could leave an orphan behind".

Dr. Ruzzi also had a fiancée and after hearing the Padre's comment he put his mind at rest and forgot all about his project of getting married in the near future.

Not much time past before he went up again to see his Spir-

---

[69] Fr. Carmelo da Sessano, Padre Pio, uomo santo di Dio by Fr Domenico Serini, Ed Pugliese, Martina Franca (TA) 2002, 13.

itual Father. After confessing him, P. Pio asked: "Why don't you get married? Long engagements ruin marriages".

He was surprised at the Saint's words, remembering what he had said to the young soldier, not less than ten days before.

However he made no objections knowing that the Padre's words were not dictated by good sense or wisdom, but came from Heaven; soon after he fixed his wedding date which took place 25 July 1943.[70]

Doubts on which to change one's mind

Although everyone respected the advice the Padre gave, it could happen that sometimes someone doubted that the Saint had the whole picture about a situation, they had mentioned in a brief chat or meeting.

Fr Pasquale Cattaneo, head of an Institution in Naples, was worried about a young priest and his lack of commitment when teaching. He spoke about it to the Padre saying he was sure the boy would have left the congregation to carry out different apostolic activities.

P. Pio disagreed and expressed his faith that the young man would be true to the promises he made when taking his vows.

When Fr. Cattaneo returned home, observing the boy's behaviour constantly he thought that P. Pio had made a mistake in his appraisal.

However the way things turned out demonstrated that the Saint was right and not him.[71]

---

[70] Angelo Ruzzi, Tolve (Pz) 18.10.1986.
[71] Father Pasquale Cattaneo, Fiera di Primiero (TN) 31.7.1988.

There was also the case where someone did not have the strength to carry out the Padre's advice.

1. One day a young fiancée went to P. Pio and told him of the serious problems she and her boyfriend were having in their relationship. The Padre listened and after a while he said: "Leave him, he is not made for you."

She returned home but she didn't have the courage to break off with her fiancée. They continued to see each other but their relationship deteriorated until the boy left her.

The young lady went back to the Padre, feeling desperate. When her turn arrived she went into the confessional booth, but as soon as the Padre saw her, he said: "You did what you wanted, now clear off."[72]

2. A girl fell in love with an Army Officer who became deaf during bombing in the Second World War. Her aunt, a spiritual daughter of the Padre wanted to talk about this to P. Pio, and he advised her it wasn't a good idea. The girl however did not want to listen to reason and she got married.

After a few days Wanda Sellach told the Padre that Cettina S., the wife, had left her husband due to the continuous tension caused by his deafness. P. Pio listened and said: "Didn't she think about this before? Didn't she know?"

"Yes, Padre, even you advised her against this marriage".

The Saint replied: "Free advice is not appreciated".[73]

3. A man in the police force was working in Foggia, but to advance his career began to play with the idea of transferring to Rome.

[72]   Ippolita Ricciardi, Foggia 22.12.1998
[73]   Wanda Sellach, San Giovanni Rotondo 19.12.1996.

One day whilst at San Giovanni Rotondo, he wanted to speak to the Padre about his problem. "But where are you going?! You are fine here advised P. Pio".

He did go to Rome, but as the Saint had foreseen, he was not happy there.[74]

5. Knowledge of languages which he had not studied

In the first volume of P. Pio's Letters, which contains the Saint's correspondence with his spiritual directors, it can be noted that Fr. Agostino Daniele from San Marco in Lamis wrote to him letters in Latin (4), in Greek (3) and in French (37); this reveals, as his confrères who edited the publishing of the Letters said, "a curious aspect and perhaps unique in spiritual correspondence: that is make use of a particular language which displeases Satan!"[75]

The epistolary contains two postcards from P. Pio written correctly in French (4-5 September and 28 November 1912), and you can read some phrases in the same language in another three letters. (1 May 1912; 20 May 1912 and 26 August 1912).

Also there must have been some preceding writings which we do not know about, if Fr. Agostino on 3 February 1912 in amazement asked P. Pio, who had not studied languages: "Who taught you French?" And the Saint, later on, 1 May 1912 wrote: "To your question about French I will answer with

---

[74] A testimony from a prayer group meeting. Comiso 21.11.1996.

[75] Padre Pio of Pietrelcina, Letters I, Correspondence with his spiritual directors (1910-1922) by Melchiorre da Pobladura and Alessandro da Ropabottoni. Ed. "Padre Pio da Pietrelcina", S. Giovanni Rotondo, 1971, 83.

Jeremiah: "A, a, a,,,nescio loqui" (Behold I cannot speak). (J. 1,6).[76]

He had not studied Greek either and yet understood and answered the letters written in this language. At the foot of the Saint's letter dated 7 September 1912, in answer to the first letter from Fr Agostino, expressed in Greek, the priest Fr. Salvatore Pannullo added: "When I asked him how he was able to read and explain it, without even knowing the Greek alphabet, he answered: "You know how! My Guardian Angel explained everything to me".[77]

In another letter dated 20 September 1912, P. Pio attributed all to the assistance of his Guardian Angel who was "the master in explaining other languages".[78]

With regards to the ability to express himself in other languages he had not studied, we wish to give the following examples.

1. In 1939 an English lady came to San Giovanni Rotondo. She knew Count John Telfener and asked him to arrange a meeting with the Padre to whom she wished to open her heart, as she had just lost a son in an accident.

Count Telfener, who was a true gentlemen, said he was very sorry he could not help her as he had to leave for Perugia to attend his wife Rina's father's funeral. He entrusted her to Elena Bandini who was fluent in English.

The gentle kind Elena accepted this task willingly and went up with the heart-broken mother to the friary. She spoke to P. Pio who told her to let the woman into his confessional.

---

[76] P. Pio quoted what the prophet answered God who declared him prophet of the nations. Cfr. Letters I. 227.

[77] Letters I, 341 note 2.

[78] Letters I, 343 see Intro Letters I 83-84.

The lady went to the forward part and spoke without the obstacle of the grate between herself and the Saint. At the end of their conversation the poor woman appeared visibly comforted and said the Padre has assured her that her son had saved his soul."[79]

2. Another testimony offered to us by Fr. Costantino Capobianco, the official reporter of the friary of San Giovanni Rotondo who has already given us lots of information on various subjects, clearly states that P. Pio had understood and spoken English on other occasions.

This episode was given to him by Angelina Serritelli.

She writes:

"Angelina's brother, Tommasino, who lived in America, after the death of his wife remarried and had a daughter. When she was old enough to make her first holy Communion, he brought her by plane to Italy, so she could receive this sacrament from the hands of P. Pio.

The young girl knew no Italian. To complete her preparation if it was necessary Tommasino and Angelina entrusted her to Mary Pyle.

The day before the first holy communion, Mary Pyle who knew what to do, took the young girl to P. Pio saying to him: "Father, I have brought Angelina's niece to confess".

"All Right".

"Father, I am here to help her because the young girl doesn't understand Italian".

"Maria, you can go because me and the young girl will see to everything".

After confession Mary who had waited for the girl asked her: "Did you understand P. Pio?".

---

[79] Rina Giostrelli, wid. Telfener, San Giovanni Rotondo 24.4.2004.

"Yes" she answered.

"And how did he speak?..In English?"

"Yes, In English"

And she repeated to Mary what the Padre had said to her.[80]

3. Fr Costantino in the Chronicle of the friary of San Giovanni Rotondo gives us the following notes which refer to the Second World War:

"12 December 1943.

Many English Officers and soldiers were present at P. Pio's Mass. They confessed and took Holy Communion. In the afternoon American officers and soldiers came (f.190)

"25 June 1944.

From various camps in Puglia American and English officers and soldiers came in a larger number than usual. A lot of them confessed and took Holy Communion.

The reporter does not specify who these soldiers confessed to, but some friars who lived with the Saint in that period of the war, assure us that P. Pio confessed some soldiers who spoke English.

We are referring to what we have heard, but a testimony from Mary Pyle tells us that our confrères have documents that back up what they say.

Mary had spoken of this to her friend Dorothy who in a publication of hers wrote: "A lot of soldiers (American) went to confess to P. Pio. You could ask how this could be, seeing that only a few soldiers spoke Italian and P. Pio didn't know

---

[80] Fr. Costantino Capobianco "Words and Anecdotes", Ed Padre Pio of Pietrelcina, San Giovanni Rotondo 1971, 129-130.

English. And yet when Mary asked them as they returned from confession "how they managed to confess if P. Pio didn't speak English", they replied: "That is his business. He told us what we needed to know". [81]

4. Fr Agostino Daniele of San Marco in Lamis writes in his *Diario*:

"Today the following fact is reported to me. In 1940 or 1941 a Swiss Priest came to see the Padre. He spoke in Latin to the Padre.

Before leaving, the priest took the liberty of asking P. Pio to pray for a sick person. The Padre answered in German: "*Ich werde sie an die gottliche Barmheizkeit empfehlen*" (I will entrust her to the Divine Mercy). The priest was astonished on hearing German and told the people who were giving him hospitality about it".[82]

With regards to expressions in idioms unknown to P. Pio we wish to refer two enjoyable episodes given to us by Probo Vaccarini, from the church of S. Martino in Venti (Rimini).

1. A woman from S. Mauro Pascoli (FO) came to San Giovanni Rotondo. She was rather old and didn't know a single word of Italian as she spoke in dialect. However she wished to confess to the Saint. She told Anita. A woman from Romagna who she was staying with: "I can't speak Italian, he speaks "giagianese"[83], how on earth will we understand each other?"

---

[81] Dorothy M. Gaudiose, "Mary l'Americana". La vita di Mary Pyle all'ombra di Padre Pio, Ed. San paolo 1995, 117.

[82] Fr. Agostino, San Marco in Lamis, "Diario" 126.

[83] In slang: dialect, unknown language.

Anita told her to prepare well for confession, but she again repeated: "But how will we manage?"

The day of her confession arrived and the country woman neared the confessional but instead of thinking about her sins murmured to herself: "Now what should I say"" When P. Pio opened the grate and asked her in dialect: "*Quand chle' che tan ti cunfes?*" (how long is it since your last confession?).

The woman hearing the dialect of S. Mauro was amazed and thinking it was a joke leaned forward to pull back the confessional curtain to see if it was really P. Pio speaking. And the Padre always speaking in the dialect of Romagna: "*Sa fet... bus, bus, invece ad cunfset?*" ("What are you doing, looking at me instead of confessing?").

The poor woman returned to the pension and from a distance shouted to Anita who was waiting to know how things had gone: "*Nita, Nita! As sem capi in tot*" (We both understood all). And after repeating exactly what had taken place she added: "*Nit a che roba cus ved, qua zo*" (Anita what a strange thing!What strange things happen down here).[84]

2. Probo Vaccarini, after getting to know P. Pio, as soon as he had some free time, took the train on which he travelled freely as he worked for the national Railways, and went to the Saint to take him his and other people's troubles. In doing so he called himself P. Pio's commuter.

One year for all Saints day and the Commemoration of Our Dearly Departed, he wished to pop in and see the Padre "to recharge his flat batteries" as he said.

The evening before he left, he said to his wife Anna Maria:

---

[84] Fr. Probo Vaccarini, Rimini 14.5.1998. Episod reported in "Anch'io pendolare" 27.

"Now I'm going to the Padre to tell him the same stories. That I do everything quickly and get myself in a state and then cause problems." Then jokingly in Romagna dialect "*La gata fretulosa la fa i gatein zegh*" the cat in a hurry has blind kittens).

In the morning he took the train to Foggia, and on his arrival at San Giovanni Rotondo, as the number of people who had booked to confess to P. Pio was relatively small he was able to confess.

The first sin he confessed was that of haste, indicating the problems that followed. The Padre looked at him benevolently and in the dialect of Romagna said: "*La gata fretulosa la fa i gatein zegh*".

Probo was astonished and looking the Padre in the eyes would have liked to say something, but he couldn't because the Saint continued: "Anything else?"[85]

6. Prophetic foretelling

It is in the gift of prophecy, we have seen, the announcement of God's word by the prophet, but according to St Thomas Aquinais, "the knowledge of each hidden thing and more precisely the news of things still to happen, belong to him.[86]

We wish to open the paragraph with a note from the Chronicle of the Friary of San Giovanni Rotondo. The reporter writes: "During lunch P. Pio with his extraordinary simplicity, recalled with reference to the opening of the friary of Pietrelcina, one of

---

[85] Ibid. this second episode can be read at page 171-172 of the same work by father Probo.

[86] SCARAMELLI *Dottrina* 245 note 2.

his prophecies. "One day I was walking with Father Tore, the archpriest of Pietrelcina, and passing by where the friary now stands, I said: "Fr Tore, one day there will be a friary here".

And he "What? go on!...more correctly "What are you talking about?".

I answered "I say they will build a friary here".

P. Pio added to his confrères: "Fr Tore didn't believe me, but now it's true isn't it?".

It should be noted the prophecy was made when P. Pio was at his family home, because doctors had advised him to go there for his health, that is 35 years ago.[87]

It is useful to give some exact data. P. Pio came to Pietrelcina the first months of 1909, and remained owing to his ill health until February 17, 1916.

The first stone of the friary, dedicated to The Holy Family was laid in 1926 by Mgr Luigi Lavitrano, the Archbishop of Benevento. However when the building was finished the friars did not have the permission from the Ecclesiastical Authorities to "take possession".

The Capuchins could only open the friary on 5 July 1947. The reporter's note was written two days after the occurrence.

P. Pio speaking to Father Salvatore Pannullo, who doubted his words, to give a reason for what he affirmed said "he had heard a choir of Angels singing and bells that rang out, "indicating with his hand a place not far away on the right of the road they were walking down".[88]

Here are other examples of Prophetic foretelling.

---

[87]   Chronicle...7 July 1947 ff 234-235.
[88]   Fr. Leonardo Treggiani, *I conventi dei Cappuccini di Foggia*, 1979, 12.01.21.

1. Emilia F was a beautiful Italian girl who in 1948 lived in Mogadiscio. A certain d'Addetta from San Giovanni Rotondo, a civil servant fell in love with her and started to court her, but she was not interested. When he returned back to his homeland the unhappy lover spoke to P. Pio asking if he should keep trying with the romance. The Padre answered; "She's not for you. She's destined to a scoundrel. When she regrets her choice it will be too late".

And so it was. During the marriage the woman discovered her husband thought nothing of the family and they were unable to live together. They separated and lost sight of each other.

Emilia herself gave us this testimony and sadly confessed: "I don't know where or who he is with".[89]

2. Some girls from San Giovanni Rotondo went to a Franciscan Youth Congress. They met and made friends with people. They met a woman from Trieste who wanted to hear about P. Pio.

One day she confided: "I never confess because the people around the confession hear all your sins". When the congress was over she wanted the address of the girls lucky enough to see the Saint.

The girls went home and after a few days a letter arrived at the "Gifra" Association at San Giovanni Rotondo from the woman asking urgently for prayers for her health; her aorta vein was causing her serious problems.

Nannina, one of the girls she had met, went to the friary and spoke to P. Pio, who told her severely: "Tell her she turned to me to heal her body not her soul. She should forget about all

---

[89] Emilia F. Taranto 31.5.1999.

the rubbishy magazines she has at home and read books about the Saints. She should say the rosary every day, because she is still in time to save her soul, she has only a month to live".

The young girl bravely gave this answer to the woman.

After a few months the woman's husband came to San Giovanni Rotondo and thanked P. Pio for his intervention, saying his wife had died just recently. P. Pio embraced him and said: "She was just in time".[90]

3. Teresa Venezia went to P. Pio in 1954 to be helped to choose her future life: whether she should get married, become a nun or stay single: her brother who was in the seminary to become a priest could have needed her. She asked the Saint what to do.

"Stay, stay as you are, he will need you", answered the Padre without a moments hesitation.

"And what if he doesn't become a priest?", asked Teresa.

"I told you to stay as you are", firmly replied P. Pio.

Teresa's doubt was legitimate, her brother still had six years to go before becoming a priest and she wanted to decide about her future with certainty.

And the Padre gave it to her, drawing on the light that came to him from the Holy Spirit. Domenico Venezia, in fact, was ordained priest 28 August 1960, and after gaining his Degree in Theology at the Lateranense University of Rome, he was the parish priest of Genzano di Lucania and spiritual father of the seminary of Potenza. His sister Teresa stayed at his side consecrating her life to the Glory of God.[91]

---

[90] Immacolatina and Giovanna Russo san Giovanni Rotondo 2.12.1985

[91] Teresa Venezia, Tolve (PZ) 18.10.1986. Fr Domenico Venezia, born in Tolve 25.11.1934 after being ordained priest, asked P. Pio's advice as to how to continue his studies. The Padre answered he should continue but

4. Luciano Livellara after a brief stay in San Giovanni Rotondo had to return to Milan for his job. Before he left he asked the Padre's blessing. P. Pio became serious and then said: "Go slowly!"

"Father, I don't race generally" observed Luciano.

And the Saint: "Go slowly and be careful I said!"

This spiritual son left driving more carefully that usual. At Ancona he stopped to have something to eat. He had just started travelling again at no more that 30 km per hour, when in a built up area a boy ran out into the middle of the road.

Livellara pulled his brakes on with all his strength. The car swerved and landed not less than half a metre from the frightened boy. Livellara's thoughts flew to the Padre. [92]

5. Our confrère Fr Atanasio Lonardo from Teano writes:

"We were in chorus for the evening oration and meditation. When the superior gave the signal to end the Communal prayers, P. Pio said: "Let us pray for our fr Provincial who is in agony".

We knew that Fr. Bernando from Apicella was ill with bronchial pneumonia, but we didn't know how seriously ill he was. Our prayers increased. The day after, 31 December 1937, we knew of his death.

After some months P. Pio assured us that he had gone to Heaven. [93]

---

warned him: "Scientia inflate" (Science swells, makes one arrogant).

[92]   Luciano Livellara, Chiavari 6.12.1994.

[93]   Testimony written by Fr Atanasio Lonardo. When the brother lived this episode he was a theology student.

6. Rosaria Balacco states: "I was 25 and my mother was 65. One day I said to the Padre I was afraid of being left alone if my mother died. P. Pio answered: "She certainly is going to live a long time. It's probable you will die first!"

My mother died aged 96, more than thirty years after my conversation with the Saint".[94]

7. Fr Eugenio Bartieri, capuchin friar from the provincial monastery of Reggio Calabria-Catanzaro states: "I went to San Giovanni Rotondo with a confrère, who was not a cleric, but because he was a friar, expected to be privileged and proceed others to talk to P. Pio. He managed to get near to him, but when he came back to me I realised things hadn't gone quite well. I didn't verify if my impression was right or not, and he didn't say anything about what had happened.

After some years that friar had some misunderstandings or contrasts with his superiors and decided to leave the Order and return to his family.

We met some years later and as he had always had a good relationship with me he opened up and confided the reasons why he had had to leave the friary.

At the end without even acknowledging any fault on his own part he said: "P. Pio was right. Do you remember when we went together to San Giovanni Rotondo and I did all I could to speak to him? Well, he treated me badly and said: "You will not die wearing this habit."[95]

8. Fr Elia De Martino from Serracapriola, capuchin priest, when he was a theology student at Campobasso, fell seriously

---

[94] Rosaria Bacco , San Giovanni Rotondo, 3.4.1996.
[95] Fr Eugenio Bartieri, capuchin. Chiaravalle Centrale (CZ) 5.8.1996.

ill with tuberculosis. During the holidays his superiors sent him to San Giovanni Rotondo "for some fresh air", they said; but as a matter of fact they were sending him away because they wished to limit the risk of infection for the other students, his companions.

In the third year of illness, in July 1940 before sending him to the Gargano, they didn't hide the seriousness of his illness which could have taken him to the grave in a short time.

In the friary the young friar helped as best he could. He took part in the communal moments of the fraternity and in the refectory or the choir he could enjoy the presence of Padre Pio who when he saw him was cordial and smiling.

Fr Elia confessed: "P. Pio looked after me more than the Fr Guardian or the others. Being aware of his confrères' needs, it was he who called the doctors. I, Instead of feeling calm because of his interest, worried more. One day when I was feeling particularly sad I decided to confess to him to receive a word of comfort.

"Father, everyone says that I am done for, that I have to die".

"Who has to die?", asked the Saint.

"Me, Father. I have tuberculosis".

And P. Pio looking at me with a reassuring smile wittily said: "Ah, you have to die? You've got a long way to go my son!"

Brother Elia returned to his theology studies and 12 June 1941 was ordained priest. He ended his days after a hardworking life, 10 February 2003 in the Friars' infirmary at San Giovanni Rotondo at the fine old age of 87.[96]

---

[96] Fr. Elia De Martino, San Giovanni 6.12.1997.

9. During the Second World War, after the armistice of September 1943, whilst the Germans withdrew towards the North, the front line arrived at Irpinia. At the end of the same month some allied soldiers camped in the garden of the Capuchin Friary of Montefusco (AV).

One night German planes bombed this enemy position.

The brothers took refuge in the cellars and were saved, but the next morning some young clerical students of philosophy who were afraid, decided to leave from the firing line. Without permission from their superior they left, some going to nearby friaries, others back home to join their families.

As soon as the provincial, Father Agostino from San Marco in Lamis heard of this, he decided that the students who had taken the initiative had to be expelled from the Order. Amongst these was the name of Terenzio Farina even though he repenting had gone back to the friary the same day he had run away. The father director, Fr Carmelo from Sessano, communicated the superiors' order and the boy was sent to his family.

He sadly took the road to Foggia, climbing on an American military lorry. But arriving at the town, instead of continuing to Cerignola, he went to San Giovanni Rotondo feeling the need to ask the Padre's protection in such a difficult moment of his life.

He arrived at the friary around 11.00 o'clock, when Padre Pio had just finished confessing the women and had just returned to cell n. 5. The boy knocked at the door which was opened to him by Fr. Pietro Tartaglia, who had come to say hello to the Padre, before going to Rome to enrol in the faculty of Canon Law, at the Gregorian University of Rome.

The young cleric was deeply moved when P. Pio hugged him and with tears in his eyes said how bitterly sorry he was to leave the habit of St Francis. He felt his vocation for the religious life too strongly to abandon it so easily.

The Padre listened, not looking at all worried. At the end he smiled and said to him: "Have your superiors told you to go back home? Well, you must obey them. Surely going back to your mother doesn't mean you have to renounce your vocation. Do you know I was at home for years with my family and yet I stayed in the Order. Go peacefully because you will be a priest".

Heartened by the Saint's words the poor exile brother Terenzio went to Cerignola, his home town, but before going to his house he went to the friary to the father guardian Fr Paolino from Casacalenda, a good man with a merciful heart. He told him his story and his meeting with P. Pio.

The good friar who knew the value of our holy brother's words, as he had been with him for some years as superior at San Giovanni Rotondo, said: "Did P. Pio tell you to be at peace with the family? Well, you do as he said".

The young man listened to his advice and serenely reached his family at home.

After about a year in November 1944, Fr Paolino was nominated provincial father for the religious Province of Foggia. Brother Terenzio returned to the friary, finished his studies and was ordained priest 27 march 1949 and in November left for the mission the capuchin Friars had in Africa. He spent twenty-two years between Eritrea and Ethiopia with confrères from Milan and CIAD, helping the poorest and needy.

P. Pio had seen far ahead.[97]

---

[97]   Fr Terenzio Farina, San Giovanni Rotondo July 1998. Died in san Giovanni Rotondo 8 May 2004.

10. Fr Gian Battista Lo Monaco offered us some notes written down by him on paper soon after a meeting he had with the Padre, who reassured him about his future.

"26 April 1939.

In the choir of the friary, 14.40. I said to the Padre: "The sky is cloudy. Let's hope we don't have thunder and lightening: "I get frightened".

The Padre: "You mustn't be afraid of lightening, because you won't die struck by lightening".

In the meantime we went down into the garden and a big dog came up to us. P. Pio shielded me saying: "Get behind me! You mustn't be afraid of lightening, but of this yes!"

"3 March 1940, 18.30.

I told the Padre of the fright I had 15 January in Palermo during the earthquake. The Padre: "Don't worry, you won't die under the rubble".

"4 March 1940, 11.45.

As I had to leave for America I begged the Padre to pray for me saying: "I don't want to end up like Jonah, swallowed by a whale!"

The Padre answered: "have no fear, you won't drown!"

"9 July 1962

I said to P. Pio: "I celebrated one of my first Masses at San Giovanni Rotondo in 1937 and here I'd like to celebrate my 25th year of priesthood".

And he: "Very good! I'll hear your Mass".

After the celebration which took place a few days later 12 July, Padre Pio congratulating me said: Well, you can book for your 50th; I won't be there but you will".

The Padre's words fixed a date to wait for: 12 July 1987. But in December 1962, after only seven years from the conversation with the Saint, Fr Gian Battista Lo Monaco had a heart attack. However it was only a cog in the wheel, because after an excellent recovery the priest returned to work at full rhythm in the Lord's garden.

When his jubilee year appeared on the horizon in the first days of January 1987, Fr Giovanni Battista's health was shook up. His blood pressure was high and he was worrying so much that the cardiologist prescribed complete rest, medicine and a special diet.

The good priest for some months did not leave home, thinking more of preparing himself to meet God, than of his Gold Jubilee.

Spring however heartened him.

26 April 1987 in his home town of Castledaccia (PA), a monument to Padre Pio was inaugurated: Fr Lo Monaco couldn't miss the occasion to pay homage to his spiritual father. His strength was weak but he was determined to go.

I, who had gone to San Giovanni Rotondo for the ceremony, found myself at his side during Mass. After Mass I joyfully listened to Fr Gian Battista who spoke about the Padre to me.

He told me many details about his meetings with the Saint, he spoke of his "Book for your 50th Mass at San Giovanni Rotondo". However, he ended sadly: "I really don't think I'll be able to make it…I don't believe I'll be able to satisfy the Padre's and my wish. July is near at hand…my strength is fading…the journey is long..".

I listened fraternally and at the end said: "Keep calm, dear Fr Gian Battista, you will surely celebrate your golden Jubilee at San Giovanni Rotondo. If, as you say, P. Pio three times expressly said as he did you can be sure he even saw your illness.

I am certain it will be and I too will be present at your Jubilee party".

12 July 1987, Fr Lo Monaco was at San Giovanni Rotondo to celebrate his Jubilee and I was at the altar as I had promised at Casteldaccia.

This spiritual son of the Padre, an active and zealous priest, serenely ended his earthly life 28 March 1999 at the good old age of 87, being born 19th March 1912.[98]

11. Sister Eliana Petrezzelli from Corato states: "I was at San Giovanni Rotondo in the years 1960-62 to attend a nursing course at the boarding school of the Home for the Relief of Suffering, where I met the Apostles of the Sacred Heart Sisters who worked at Padre Pio's Hospital.

During this period the Lord let me hear his call to religious life and in a confession to P. Pio I told him my sentiments. His answer was not illuminating. He only said: "*E mo pure tu ti vuo' fa capa di pezza* (Now you too want to become a nun)?"[99].

I went home for the holidays and spoke of my idea to the family but my mum was quite against it.

Back at boarding school and being able to confess to the Padre I said one day: "Mum is being difficult about me entering the friary".

The Padre quickly soothed me saying: "You'll enter, you will enter".

Everything resolved itself. Mum dreamt of P. Pio, who she

---

[98] The notes regarding the events and words of the Padre were kindly given by Fr G.B. Lo Monaco in photocopies of notes taken by him whilst the events were taking place.

[99] Neopolitans jokingly call nuns "cape e pezza", rag heads.

didn't know, with a large host in his hands saying to her: "Let your daughter leave".

When I had finished my training as a nurse I entered the order of the Apostles of the Sacred Heart. Mother was happy and later on repeated: "You chose the best road".[100]

12. Graziano Borelli tells us:

"A Dominican priest I knew said to me one day: "When you see P. Pio ask him for me, how I must plan my spiritual direction for a soul. It's useless to add further details, if he really is a man of God he'll understand and give me the right answer".

On a visit to the Padre I referred what the priest had asked me. He answered: "He should prepare her for the great step: death."

When I returned from San Giovanni Rotondo, I gave the friar the Saint's answer.

He gave me a little smile which revealed his scepticism. After fifteen days he phoned me: the woman for whom he had asked P. Pio's advice, had died.

Graziano adds another testimony.

A couple from Florence asked the Padre some advice regarding their business: should or shouldn't they sell their Jewellery shop which was on Ponte Vecchio. P. Pio replied: "Do it as soon as possible".

They however took their time, too much time. In the 1966 November floods the angry waters destroyed all".[101]

---

[100] Sister Eliana Petrezzelli, Bari 29.4.1995.
[101] Graziano Borelli, Pistoia, 9.10.1999.

7. The gift of healing

The fame of being a healer has always accompanied P. Pio. For this also many people who suffered came to the Gargano, hoping to receive from the Saint a gesture which gave relief or a word of hope.

The touch of the healing hand

It is human gesture to put out a hand towards one's brother to express solidarity and interest, to give comfort to his pain. Driven by compassion good people do this. In saints this can be translated into effective benefits which are sometimes immediate.

The pages of the Gospel show us Jesus, God's Saint, sent to us by the Padre as our saviour who repeats this gesture: with the leper (Mk 1, 41) with the two blind men (Mt 9, 29) with the deaf and dumb man (Mk 7, 33) with the blind man of Betsaida (Mk 8,22). People had understood that a liberating force came from him, because those who touched him were cured (Mt 14, 36). So those who were ill threw themselves upon him (Mt 12,15; Lk 6, 18-19).

The Gospel scenes were seen in the Gargano around P. Pio.

The Saint, it has already been revealed, feared contact with people in church and he complained to the father guardian: "They throw themselves on me...I am aching all over my body". Therefore when he left the confessional he wanted his confrères to protect him, to shield that body of his which not only carried the stigmata of Jesus, but also suffered being flogged each morning in Holy Mass.

"People's troubles" never left him indifferent. He was aware the Holy Spirit could allow him to sooth pain, emitting the force of God, which lived in him, as in a worthy and perfect temple. It has been seen how in the confessional his hand healed.[102]

To the cases already reported, we wish to add a few more.

1. Fr Emanuele Grassi. a capuchin friar of the religious province of Bologna, often came down south, as he came from a town in Molise, Riccia. Without fail he went up to San Giovanni Rotondo to visit P. Pio.

Once he had a pain in his shoulder which was worrying him. He confessed to the Padre and told him about it: "It's been bothering me for a while. I'm a bit worried".

"No, no", said the Padre gently tapping him a few times on the part troubling him: "Don't worry". The pain disappeared and did not return.[103]

2. Mario Tentori suffered with a gastro-duodenal ulcer. One day after confession he spoke about it to P. Pio: "Father, please pray for my stomach".

"If you knew what I suffer with my stomach!" replied the Saint, but soon after added: "Yes, let us pray, let us pray!"

A year later Mario, returned to San Giovanni Rotondo and after confession said: "Father a doctor told me that I have to have an operation for my stomach ulcer".

"Ah these doctors always want to cut!" replied the Saint. Then fatherly looking at this spiritual son he said: "I'll see to

---

[102] See The "Padre" part I, p.61-65.
[103] Fr Emanuele Grassi from Riccia, capuchin friar, San Giovanni Rotondo 13.11.1996.

it!". And he gave three knocks with his hand on his stomach.

Mario returned to Milan and no longer felt the sharp pains that had tormented and worried him for such a long time. Only in Spring and Autumn did he feel some slight pain, that he could easily treat with some pills.

The Padre had left him only a sign of the primitive suffering; this to keep him vigilant and grateful before God, good and merciful to his children.[104]

3. In another occasion the touch of the Saint's hand was like a rough beneficial caress.

One Renata from Parma came to P. Pio because since she was a child she had a pierced eardrum and pus dripped out of her ear. Doctors had advised an operation, but she didn't want to undergo any operation. And, as she heard a constant buzzing sound that drove her crazy, she wanted to die.

She spoke more than once about it to the Padre, who told her one day at the end of confession: "You have to have an operation, you really must".

She replied "But I am afraid of the pain"

"And what if I take the pain?" asked the Padre.

"Well then, yes" replied the penitent.

"Well all right then" concluded the Saint.

In the meantime Renata moved to the front of the confessional to kiss his hand and said: "Father, it is not right that you should suffer for me. I beg you, put your hand on my ear"

"But what do you want my hand to do?" replied the confessor.

"Just put it there, what will it cost you? Insisted the patient.

---

[104] Don Bruno Borelli, Erba 19.9.1998..

The Padre as if he was embarrassed gave her a little slap.

The woman felt a terrible pain, it was so bad she screamed. She ran away crying and stopped under the elm tree in the square. A lot of people gathered around her to know what had upset her so much. Someone who knew her advised her to obey the Padre and go and see a doctor. In the meantime the buzzing had disappeared.

After a few days she went to Bologna and went to see the doctor who was following her case. He examined her and pulling her ear asked her: "Where have you been, to see St Rita of Cascia?".

"No, I've been to see P. Pio in San Giovanni Rotondo", answered the woman.

"Your eardrums are perfectly healthy. There is no damage any more"

A miracle had taken place.[105]

When the Holy Spirit worked through the hand of P. Pio it could also happen out of the confessional.

Here are some examples:

1. Andrea Cardinale gave us this statement.

"My dad, Bernardino Cardinale. Had an operation in Rome: they had removed one lung completely and half the other lung. His red corpuscles were lower than necessary. The doctors at the end of the operation told my mum to take him to Bari so he could die at home.

You can imagine how my poor mother felt. One day, going through her handbag she unexpectedly found a photo of P. Pio in her hands and decided to take the sick man to San Giovanni

---

[105] *Notes*...San Giovanni Rotondo, May 1993..

Rotondo. She knew Dr Giovanni Delfino and asked him to introduce her husband to the Padre.

After the good doctor had quietly said a few words about the case to P. Pio, my father said to the Saint: "Father, am I going to live? Will I work again? I can't die, I have a six year old son!"

P. Pio banging his hand several time on the patient's chest replied: "You'll live, you'll work…and how much you'll work!"

The sick man decided to stay in San Giovanni Rotondo. After four months being there he said: Father, I must go back to Bari. It's Christmas, I have to go and see my son, he's ill."

And the Padre: "But no, he's not ill, your son is well".

My dad moved away, but to the father superior he bumped into said: "This morning P. Pio didn't understand me. I've heard from Bari that my son is ill and he instead said he's not ill at all".

The friar replied: "Look here it's you that haven't understood P. Pio".

To make sure of what was happening he went to personally phone home and they answered that in truth I no longer had a high temperature.

Naturally enough my father didn't move from San Giovanni Rotondo and asked my mother to come up to the Gargano with me. So we all had Christmas together with P. Pio.[106]

2. Wanda Cettolin tells us:

"I met P. Pio between 1960-61. Ida Sellach, a friend of mine who often went to San Giovanni Rotondo on hearing that my

---

[106]   Andrea Cardinale, Campitello Matese (CB) 2.3.1995.

dad was ill and much weakened by a serious haemorrhage which had lasted over two weeks without stop, invited me to go down to see the Padre. I agreed and we left the day after on a bus for pilgrims; my husband in the meantime had written a letter for me to give to P. Pio.

We stopped at the Loreto Shrine, so that the pilgrims could attend Mass. As I went in I saw at the door a friar with big dark eyes who was staring at me: his gaze made me feel uncomfortable. I stopped a while and he kept on looking at me. At the end of the Mass I didn't see him any more.

We continued the journey. At the first bend in the road going up to San Giovanni Rotondo I felt sick, so sick that I called for help. Ida said: "Take courage Wanda, we are nearly there".

When we arrived at the square in front of the friary we went towards the church and there I met P. Pio for the first time: he was the friar I had seen of the threshold at the Loreto Shrine, who had stared at me for so long. To Ida who was able to kiss his hand he said: "At last my daughter, at last you have finally arrived!".

We attended the Eucharistic Benediction that evening. I was at the side of the altar. When the Padre lifted the Sacrament of Jesus to bless us, I fell to the ground. To those who wanted to lift me up the Saint shouted: "Leave her alone" and added: "take her to Saint Michael".

We went the next day to the Shrine of Monte Sant'Angelo, but even there during Mass I collapsed on the floor.

Before we left San Giovanni Rotondo, Ida Sellach said to me: "P. Pio wishes to see you" and the door keeper allowed me to go in the cloisters near the opening where P. Pio would have entered. He arrived soon after and seeing me so upset said: "Why are you crying?".

I, in giving him the letter said: "My dad is dying!". P. Pio said: "Woman of little faith, your dad is cured, but it is you who are ill".

In truth I was troubled with sinus. Also when I spoke my neck swelled due to a cist which pushed forwards. Then the Padre said: "Lower your head!".

I did so and he gave me three strong taps with his fingertips and said: "*You may go all over the world but you will always be my spiritual daughter*. Now however go to hospital quickly".

"Father, but I have to leave with the others, I have to go home".

"Go to hospital, I said", replied the Padre. He blessed me and closed the door behind him.

When I left the friary I phoned home and the family assured me my father's haemorrhage had stopped. At the time he was 60 years old: he lived until he was 81.

In the meanwhile I went to the Home for the Relief of Suffering where I asked to be examined. When the doctor came he found me in tears and asked: "Why are you crying?".

"P. Pio has sent me here, perhaps I need an operation on my neck" I answered.

"Let's have a look" he said.

Then after a careful examination he added: "But what do you need to be operated on?"

I, wishing to show him the swelling, realised that my neck had become normal again. "Can't you see that P. Pio operated on you whilst you were coming here" said the doctor, and allowed me to leave.

I went back into church. It was five o'clock and the Padre was giving Blessing. After our group had said goodbye, he looked at me with his profound gaze and smiled. We left.

I arrived home and the operation was not mentioned again, even if I had some slight problems. Today 18 September 1997

I can say: The Padre relieves but leaves you in the company of sufferance.

I thought many times about P. Pio's words "You may go all over the world…". What did he mean? It all became clear when my husband said soon after that due to work we had to go to Brazil where we stayed for ten years.

One day when I was tidying the room, I could smell a strong perfume, then the door flew open and I saw P. Pio dressed for Holy Mass. It was a flash, a single instant. I switched on the radio and heard that unfortunately the Padre had died.[107]

His intercession

Generally it was through prayer that the Padre bent God's heart to intervene to help the suffering, without adding any external gesture.

1. Angelo Cantarelli, from Parma, went down to San Giovanni Rotondo when his firm was having difficulties: he wanted to speak about this to the Saint. He could only do so in the confessional.

He gathered from people what was said about the severity and judgement of that exceptional confessor and realised that one needed to be well prepared and that the Padre didn't accept general accusations of sins committed. He tried to clearly think of his past, but found himself in difficulty to put together all the errors of a life without participating in the sacraments.

When he knelt at P. Pio's feet, he began saying: "Father, I am full of sins, all except murder. However I repent all and I

---

[107] Wanda Cettolin, Erba (Co) 18.9.1997.

wish to start a new life". The Padre listened to his confession, asked him a few questions and particulars and gave him absolution. The penitent was incredulous at his indulgence and said to the Saint: "Father, did you understand me?".

And the Saint: "What do you mean, have I understood you?! And in your opinion I'd give you absolution like that?... without understanding you?".

His conversion was a true one. He went to Mass and communion every day and was charitable to the poor. He became a spiritual son of P. Pio. He often went down from Parma to take offerings for P. Pio's "Home for the Relief of Suffering" project of which he was a great benefactor.

Once after staying a few days with his spiritual father, he took the train at Foggia station to go home but during the journey he had a stroke which left him paralysed. The train made an emergency stop and the patient was taken to the clinic "Villa dei Pini" near Civitanova Marche.

In the meantime the news reached San Giovanni Rotondo and the Padre sent Enzo Bertani from the board of directors of the "Home of the Relief of Suffering" to take comfort to the sick man and his family.

After a few days, Enzo returned to San Giovanni Rotondo and telling the Padre of the pain and complaints from the children and wife of the patient with regards to the "lack of help" from the Saint for such a dear son" he said: "Father, you must obtain the grace of full recovery for him. In Parma they are sadly saying he went to P. Pio to take charity for the sick and he got thrombosis!"

It was evening. The Padre listened, much saddened he said nothing.

The following day, at the end of the Holy Mass, the Saint begged Bertani to go once more to Civitanova: "Tell the family to be calm, I've asked the Lord to let him have another ten years of life".

After two weeks Angelo came out of his deep coma and returned home. In a short while he was back to normal, carrying out his business. At the time indicated by P. Pio the Lord called him to Heaven.[108]

2. It is sister Pura Pagani who speaks to us.

"I had planned a trip to see P. Pio again, but before leaving I wished to go and say hello to Fr. Giancarlo Stella, priest at Cavazzale (VI) who was in hospital with lung cancer. The sick man asked me to mention him to the Holy Friar: "Tell the Padre about my illness".

When I arrived in San Giovanni Rotondo, together with some other people they let me into the corridor of the friary where the Saint would pass by. I was lost in my thoughts when he arrived. He gave me his hand to kiss and I was able to tell him some problems. Before ending our short conversation the Padre asked "Anything else to tell me?".

I was rather surprised by his question but then I pulled myself together and said "Ah yes Father, our parish priest is ill with a tumor and he'd like a word from you".

P. Pio: "And if God has decided he must die, what does he want?"

"Father, to get better. Father, he wants to get better".

The Saint remained silent for a while and then "Well let's let go ...." he said without ending the phrase. When I got home I learnt that Gianfranco had left the hospital. I went to presbytery to tell him what the Padre said. He never set foot in hospi-

---

[108] Enzo Bertani, San Giovanni Rotondo, 4.12.1995.

tal again and today after thirty years, he is still alive.[109]

3. Mimmo, Ignazio and Lucia Merendino's first son, always had a headache. After any activity, playing or doing something, he would stop and hold his head saying: "Mum I've got a headache, a splitting headache". Then he would sit down feeling depressed.

His mother wanted to take him to the doctor's, but his father said: "No I'm taking him to San Giovanni Rotondo to see P. Pio" and he left. When he saw the Padre he asked him what he should do for his son. He answered: "Take him to see a good doctor. I'll pray that the Lord will help him to make a good diagnosis".

Ignazio was not at all satisfied and asked Maria Tagliavia to speak to the Padre again for him. The good spiritual daughter did so: "Father, the sick boy's father won't have the child visited by any doctor, he won't take him anywhere. He wants you to do everything. Please, you see to it."

P. Pio listened, raised his eyes and then after a minutes silence said "Very well."

Mimmo never had a headache again.[110]

4. Lucia Merendino from Salemi, Mimmo's mother told us.

"I was expecting my sixth child. I confessed to P. Pio and at the end I said "Father I'm expecting a baby. Please bless it." He didn't answer me. I looked at him through the confessional grate and saw that he was immobile staring upwards.

I repeated my prayer: "Father I'm expecting a baby, please bless it!" As before the Padre gave me no answer.

[109] Sister Pura Pagani, Mozzecane (VR) 10.5.1997.
[110] Lucia Merendino, Salemi (TR) 2.11.1996.

For third time I repeated my request imploring him: "Father, I'm pregnant, I'm having a baby. Please bless it!" And he clearly pronounced the words "And I bless it for you".

In the meantime, since we had built a little chapel in the country, I asked if we should dedicate it to Our Lady and with which title. He almost stopped me from speaking saying "To Our Lady's mother, St. Anne".

"But Padre, we were thinking of Our Lady!"

"To Our Lady's mother, St. Anne!" he repeated forcefully. Then I remembered that St. Anne is the patron Saint of women in labour.

That evening I attended Mass at the end of which P. Pio blessed all people present with Jesus in the Blessed Sacrament. Whilst the Padre made the sign of the cross over us, I fell to the ground; but after a few minutes I came round. The days went by and I no longer felt any sign of life with in me .At the end of nine months I went into labour, and gave birth to a decomposed badly formed little girl. Those assisting me were amazed I had managed to carry a baby in that condition for three months without serious consequences for my health; according to medical science I should have died of blood poisoning.[111]

5. Sister Eleonora Di Carlo states.

"One day, I don't remember exactly when, but it was in 1963, my brother from Potenza gave me some bad news, my mother had had a stroke and the doctors thought she would not recover.

We sisters of the Home for the Relief of Suffering had the privilege of giving P. Pio Easter greetings during Holy Week.

---

[111] Lucia Merendino, Salemi (TR) 2.11.1996.

Taking the opportunity of being near to the Padre, I took his hand to kiss it and asked with my heart the grace that my mum would be cured, but with my voice only prayers.

He listened, looked at me with his heavenly eyes and said "Very well".

My mum was cured and after a few days I went to thank him, he answered me gruffly: "Are you coming to thank me? You should go and thank our Lord Jesus Christ instead".[112]

6. Dr. Nicolino Bellantuono tells us.

"In July 1949 I had to take a medical exam at university and I asked Maria Ciaccia, one of P. Pio's spiritual daughters to ask the Padre, when she went to see him, a prayer for me. At the end of confession she told the Saint about my request.

P. Pio answered: "It will go well, it will go well!". But soon after, gazing far away looking into nothing, he shouted "Poor boy, poor boy!".

Maria was very surprised, but asked nothing thinking that perhaps P. Pio was referring to someone else.

The exam went well and 17th July I returned home. After a few days I started to have severe pains in my stomach and abdomen which got stronger and stronger, I felt as if I was dying. I felt as though I had a perforation. All night I repeated; "Go to the Padre, go to the Padre!".

They gave me a sedative, but once it wore off the pain started again and I began to have hiccups and be sick.

The day after my father, who was a doctor wanted to consult his colleagues: prof. Salvatore Chiaccia, Dr. Vincenzo Ciaccia, Dr.Giovanni Borrelli. All agreed on the diagnosis: acute peritonitis. They all said there was nothing more to do.

---

[112] Sister Eleonora Di Carlo, Cassano Murge (BA) 30.6.1993.

Meanwhile my sister and my fiancée Maria left for San Giovanni Rotondo where they arrived in the morning. They heard Mass and soon afterwards went near to P. Pio and said "Father, Nicolino is dying."

"What's the matter, what has he got?" he asked most alarmed.

"The doctors say he has peritonitis and there is nothing they can do for him".

The Padre lowered his gaze looking mortified. He stayed silent for a while. Then becoming calmer he said: "Don't worry. What do you mean peritonitis? Everything will go alright." And after blessing them he went away.

Feeling encouraged and serene the women went back home and referred all the Padre had told them. From that moment I started to improve: my pain lessened as did my sickness.

After about twenty days I got up again".[113]

8. The power of miracles

Amongst the charismas that St. Paul numbers in his letters to the Corinthians is *the gift of performing miracles* (Cor. 1.12.10.) The cures of which we have spoken, are miracles worked by God through the intercession of our Saint; but, other than curing health, the Holy Spirit's intervention produced other beneficial effects such as saving life, giving life or improving living conditions.

1. Wanda Sellah says: "In November 1942, I went from Cerignola (FG) to Turin to attend the first year at St. Francis Professional Teaching school in Via Giacosa 12.

---

[113] Nicolino Bellantuono Torremaggiore 11.6.1999.

One day the town suffered carpet bombing; I ran but it seemed as if the bombs were following me. I arrived back at the boarding school, but Mother Superior advised all the boarders to leave the house which had been hit by incendiary bombs and was no longer safe for shelter.

I went out into the street to look for a safe place, but a burning object fell right in front of me: I was tempted to go back, but I didn't because several parts of the house were on fire.

It was night time but the town seemed as if it were day time due to the many fires. I saw harrowing sights; people burning alive: children on the street and mothers who died by their windows or on their balconies. I reached my uncle's house in Via Berutti 6.

A few weeks later my mother wrote to me that she had had a dream: a letter from P. Pio had arrived and when she opened it there was a note on which was written: "Come, I am down here, waiting for you! " Signed: P. Pio. There was also a drawing of a cross which looked as if it had been rubbed out.

As before I left for Turin, my mother had asked P. Pio to keep me safe, she thought that dream confirmed what she asked for.

However she wanted confirmation from the Saint and as I had returned to Cerignola, we went up to San Giovanni Rotondo together.

After confession mum told P. Pio of her dream and the bombing in Turin, in which I had been saved. She asked him, "Father, was it you who spoke to me in my dream?".

"Yes! Why? Are you surprised?".

"Father, what about that crossed out cross?".

"There is much bereavement in this world and one was for you. The Lord cancelled it".[114]

---

[114] Wanda Sellach. S.G.R. 30.11.1995.

2.   The Friary Chronicle on 23rd October 1953 reports:

"This morning Miss Amelia Zuossa, blind from birth, aged 27 from S. Nazzaro del Grappa (Vicenza) received the power to see. This is how. After confessing she asked P. Pio to be able to see; The Padre answered: " Have faith and pray a lot". Instantly the young woman saw P. Pio: his face, his blessing hand, and his half- gloves that hid his stigmata.

Her sight continued to improve until the girl saw well from close up. Telling P. Pio of this grace, he answered: "Let us thank the Lord". Then the girl whilst in the cloisters kissed the Padre's hand and thanked him, asking him to have complete vision. The Padre said " Bit by bit it will come."[115]

Faith and prayer

To obtain an extra ordinary intervention by God in our lives, prayers said in true faith as an appeal are necessary. Prayer comes spontaneously to an unhappy heart, but it is not always accompanied by the blind faith which should be given to a good Father to which nothing is impossible.

Jesus in the Gospel is moved to act by the faith in Him showed by those who asked for help; that is the case with the centurion in front of whom the Master remained "amazed" (Mt. 8, 5-13) of those who brought the bed-ridden paralytic man (Mt.9,2) and the Canaanite woman who asked that her daughter be freed from an evil spirit.(Mt. 15,28.)

The Lord called for faith from Jairus who begged him to save his daughter who was dying. (Lk 8, 50) attributing his faith to the blessing he received, saying: "Thy faith saved thee." (Mt.9, 22; Lk 7, 50 and 17,19).

---

[115]   Ibid, ff. 338-239.

P. Pio knew that God had filled his hands with graces to give to mankind; but once he said sadly to Nina Campanile: "The Lord is ready to do miracles, but there is a lack of faith".[116]

A note by the Saint with regards to the "lack of faith" in the learned men and women has a particular flavor. He observed that God, in certain environments "does not do miracles, to not make the scholars more responsible" at the moment when they will be judged by the divine court.[117]

Let us see other cases of miracles worked by the Lord for the intercession of P. Pio, who recommend to those who turn to him, to pray insistently, continuously and faithfully.

1. Guerrino Venier, born in Sedegliano di Gravisca (UD) met P. Pio in 1958. His wife Maria had a serious liver condition so he decided to go down to San Giovanni Rotondo to speak about it to the Padre.

When he arrived, he asked a friar to let them meet the Saint, as he couldn't stay away from his family for a long time. He was accompanied to P. Pio. When the two of them were in front of P. Pio the good confrère said "Father, this man would like to speak to you."

Guerrino knelt down, and told him about his wife's illness, trusting in his intercession.

The Padre, after listening to him, said "Well, well!" He gave him a tap on the head with his fingertips and added: "Go and pray!".

When Guerrino got up, he saw in front of him a giant. He

---

[116] Nina Campanile, testimony registered in San Giovanni Rotondo 15.10.1973 by Fr Saldutto.

[117] Ibid.

asked himself: "But who is this man?" After a few instants he found P. Pio in his normal shape.

When he returned to Biella he started a new life from a Christian point of view. He was already near to God but after P. Pio's call to pray, he attended the sacraments more regularly and he daily recited the rosary to Our Lady.

His wife was no longer troubled by her liver and lived for a further twenty years.[118]

2. Paola Donini from Cesenatico went down to San Giovanni Rotondo in 1964. She had been married for years and was longing for a child who showed no sign of arriving; she had gone to the Padre for a word that would bring hope to her heart. She couldn't stay the time necessary for the booking (13-15 days), but it seemed as if luck was on her side: a lady who had booked 10 days before, gave her the ticket as she had been called back home.

After a day or two Paola went to confess, but as soon as she opened the confessional window P. Pio said: "Go away, because you have jumped the queue".

Feeling humiliated in front of everyone she started to feel resentful towards the Padre. The friar, who kept everyone near the confessional in order, realized her desperation said to her: "Madam write a letter expressing your needs."

She didn't want to take his advice. "Do you really think of all the letters he receives, he'll read mine!? She said. Then persuaded she gave the merciful capuchin a note with her request.

She waited in the church and felt a great peace come into her heart; the rancor she felt towards the Saint magically dis-

---

[118] Guerrino Venier, Biella 3.12.1999.

appeared. In the afternoon the friar saw her at the foot of Our
Lady of Grace's altar and said to her: "P. Pio has read your note
and he had said to me: "Tell that woman to have more faith and
she will receive the grace of her desire."

Paola returned to Cesenatico feeling much better, but her
wish to personally speak to the holy man was so strong that
after a few months she left once more for San Giovanni Rotondo. She queued, prayed and finally after confessing was able
to express her wish personally to the Padre. "I would love to
have a child, even if I have adopted my youngest brother at my
mother's death" she said.

P. Pio: "That does not come into it. You will have a child
of your own, but you must continue to have faith and you will
receive this grace."

Mrs. Donini told us: "I went back to Cesenatico and I started to pray. The years went by, but I didn't lose hope. I said to
myself "If P. Pio said I would become a mother, sooner or later
it will happen".

And a son arrived after 18 years of marriage.[119]

3. Anna Palange widow Parisi states;

It was during the last World War in 1943, when Campobasso was occupied by German troops. The allies from the sky
during air raids dropped bombs on enemy positions. One day
one of these bombs fell near a built up area causing a large fire.
Our men who came out of hiding trying to put it out were captured by the Germans and loaded onto lorries to be deported
to Germany.

When I saw that my husband was amongst them I felt para-
lyzed and unable to say a word. I was six months pregnant and

---

[119] Paola Donini, Cesena. 14.5.1998.

my mother shook me to make me come back to my senses ; I finally managed to shout "Our Lady of Pompei." A few hours later the soldiers released our men who returned to us.

I gave birth to a son and named him Emilio, but at the age when children start speaking I realized he had difficulty in doing so. I took him to Rome for a medical examination and the doctor told me the baby had suffered a sort of foetal paralysis that had touched him " like a caress." I had other examinations done and I was advised to let the baby have an operation. As I was not at all sure of what to do, I did nothing.

In 1948 I took the baby to San Giovanni Rotondo. We arrived about 14.00; the time when P. Pio went to confess the men.

I having heard on the square near the church that a man from Val Gardena had a booking to speak to P. Pio. Entrusted my son to him so that the Padre could bless the child. Whilst the man was waiting his turn, P. Pio moved the confessional curtain and making a sign with his hands, said: "Come here!".

The Gardenese moved forward but the Padre said :"No not you, the little boy" and added: "Emilio, come here." The little boy did so, P .Pio blessed him and then continued confessing.

When the kind gentleman brought the boy back to me, he said a little resentfully: "Madam, you made me feel a bit of a fool in front of P. Pio. You entrusted the boy to me to be blessed, when the Padre already knew him, in fact he called him by name".

I assured him that in truth it was the first time that I or my son had come to San Giovanni Rotondo.

The day after I was able to confess to P. Pio but because before me he had sent an old woman away, as soon as I approached the confessional feeling very emotional I started to cry. The Padre said, "Quiet, quiet, don't cry: keep calm otherwise I won't confess you".

I calmed down as best as I could and said "Father, I have come to ask advice about my son".

And Padre Pio "For who, that little boy you sent me yesterday afternoon, for Emilio?".

"Yes Father , he does not speak clearly and they have told me to let him have an operation".

"No, no, you must not do that. Pray, pray, have faith in God and see what happens", answered the Saint.

I obeyed the Padre; the child even if he was not perfectly cured, started to express himself well. He had a normal youth, got married and managed his father's shop".[120]

4. Baldo Colavizza was presented to P. Pio through a photograph.

When he was three years old he became ill with Bone and Lung TBC. He was treated at the "Al Mare" Hospital of the Venice Lido, from 1947 to the summer of 1953 with a 6 to 9 month interval at the "Fatebene fratelli" Hospital of Gorizia.

His mother, Norina Gressani, because she was poor, could only go every so often from Tolmezzo (UD) to see her son. The doctors told her that the boy's condition was serious. In the summer of 1950 having heard that Miss Rosina and Miss Lucia Castellani because it was Holy Year, after going to Rome would have visited San Giovanni Rotondo to meet P. Pio, trusted them with her sorrowful anxiety: "I will never be able to visit that holy man to talk to him about my Baldo, because I haven't got the means to do so. I trust you to speak of his illness and suffering".

The two spiritual daughters stayed at San Giovanni Rotondo for several days and confessed to the Padre. At the begin-

---

[120] Anna Palange widow Parisi, Campitello Matese (CB) Oct.1995

ning of the confession, the Saint told Lucia to be quiet as he would have listened to her sins.

When P. Pio came out of the confessional the two sisters showed him the little boy's photo asking him to pray for his recovery and they spoke of his mother's worries.

And the Padre said: "He will get better, but his mother must pray more, because the child is praying more than she his".

At their return Norina listened much moved by what the Saint had said, and re-heartened she multiplied her prayers to God. As time passed Balbo's health started to improve until he eventually left the hospital completely cured.

He began studying and passed an exam to become a headmaster: he worked well and diligently in this role.

Whilst he was studying, and afterwards, his mother often reminded him: "You are a son of P. Pio. He cured you. You must go and thank him. He is a Saint."

Baldo confesses: "As a boy, observing the veneration my mother had for P. Pio I used to say to myself: "But aren't saints in Heaven? But then I understood that the saints are first amongst us. Gifts from God"[121]

5. As we have seen in the last case, not all those who wished to communicate with P. Pio were able to do so by going to San Giovanni Rotondo; some entrusted their requests to go-betweens. However a lot of them used the post to express their wishes and appeals for prayers.

Parcels of correspondence arrived for the Padre daily, and four or five brother friars were not always enough to go through the requests and supplications he received, or to tell him of the most serious cases. In the evening before the Padre went to

---

[121] Baldo Colavizza, San Giovanni Rotondo, 2.11.2005, day he came down to thank P. Pio.

bed he blessed the out going post that surely brought benefits at its arrival.

It would take too long to refer to this fully. We will concentrate on one case only. Barbara Antonia narrates.

"I was unable to have a child as they died after 4 or 5 months pregnancy; my friend, Nina Fiorese, advised me to write to P. Pio. I begged her to write a couple of words for me and posted the note to the Saint.

After a few days I received an answer. I opened the envelope and found a holy picture of Our Lady of Grace and one of God's servant Fr. Raffaele of Sant`Elia a Pianisi, capuchin friar; in the accompanying note were the following words: "P. Pio said: Make a novena to Our Lady of Grace and God's servant Fr. Raffaele, capuchin and your grace will be conceded". Signed: Father Guardian of the friary of San Giovanni Rotondo, 15th September 1959.

The following year a baby boy was born who is still alive and well today. In 1963 to the great joy of all the family another son was born and named Pio Cataldo.

Naturally enough I made the novena and continued to do so for a long time, and the blessing I had faithfully waited for through P. Pio's intercession arrived. I am always thankful to him for this."[122]

A brief aside. In the five cases quoted above in which P. Pio obtained favors from the Lord, we can see that in four of them the one who pleads a grace or favor is a mother.

Padre Pio's spiritual daughters are in agreement in affirming that the Saint always looked with an attentive mindful eye at the problems facing mothers. They were the Padre's privileged interlocutors.

---

[122]   Barbaba Antonia, Fasano (BR) 29.4.1991.

Irma Vinelli recounts that one day she received a telegram for a lady who asked for P. Pio's intervention because she was due to give birth; but the baby was in a difficult position. She went to the friary and at the same moment the Padre assured her of his help, the little baby was born.

It is the same Irma Vinelli who one day said to the Saint: "Father I have no milk for my baby boy!".

And he answered: " What do you mean, a mother without milk for her baby?".

Immediately her milk started to flow and she could not wait to go home.[123]

The meaning of miracles

Before we close this paragraph we wish to make some considerations to clarify the intimate value of miracles.

Let's say first of all that is in an intervention by God, which is visible and verifiable and indicates that He is present in the middle of his people and works for their well- being. It also educates Christians to see all the happenings of life in the light of faith and to live faith itself better.

"In Divine intentions, a miracle serves to break routine; it impedes that one acts in a repetitive ritualistic religious way that reduces all to "half-baked notions of human customs"; produces an examination of the conscience, keeping stupor alive which is indispensable in the relationship with God. The actual miracle helps one to grasp the habitual miracle of life and being, in which we are immersed and easily take for granted and banalize. At the same time it helps to confound

---

[123] Notes…, May 1993.

"the knowledge of the knowledgeable", that is put in a healthy crisis the pretext that reason can explain all and refuse all that is unexplainable. It breaks both ritualism and dry rationality. In a biblical sense, it serves to uplift and not to lower the quality of religiosity".[124]

Why doesn't the Lord always intervene?

Sometimes at San Giovanni Rotondo it was possible to hear someone say, in a cross between wonder and a trace of protest: "Despite all my consistent prayers said faithfully, P. Pio has not obtained the grace I asked for".

Bro Daniele Natale told the Padre of a case in which there was a similar lament. The Saint pointing his finger towards the sky, said: "It all depends on him!"[125]

The Padre's answer brings us to this consideration: even if something is good the Lord cannot always allow it, if it does not fit into His divine providence.

An example. We know that a particular illness forced P. Pio, when he was young, to live at home, away from the cloister. His superiors did all they could to take him back to the friary, but there his illness became worse than ever.

Advice from Rome was that the Capuchin Friar should become a priest. The mere idea of being cut out of St. Francis order was death to the Saint.

He turned to Our Lady to ask her to be able to live following the rules, in community like all the other friars. But the Holy Virgin, who had always reserved the most delicate care

---

[124] CANTALMESSA, *Il canto dello spirito…,* 212.
[125] Bro Daniele Natale, Cerignola 3.10.1986.

for this son, in front of his insistent pleas, as a sign of disagreement lowered her eyes or even no longer showed him "her beautiful face".[126]

It is clearly evident that what P. Pio asked for was not part of the ends, known only to God.

But we wish to stay on the subject a little longer. Sometimes it happens one meets people who after turning to God to ask him to heal their loved one find themselves facing death. So, feeling deluded they wander away from Him: they no longer pray, they do not go to church on Sunday to take part in the Eucharist.

What is there to say to these creatures?

P. Pio, to stay on the subject of sickness, gave precise indications. He said: "We all have the duty to take care of ourselves, because our health is a wealth to look after." We know in fact that the Lord gave man intelligence and capability because turning to medicine he can oppose the illnesses that strike and give remedies to cure them. The Saint however remembers that we are always in God's hands.

Once Natalino Rappa from Biella came down to San Giovanni Rotondo and meeting the Padre, she complained that she was not well and the treatment she was receiving was giving no relief.

P. Pio listened to her and then said: "Remember that doctors and medicine are effective when the Eternal Father wishes them to be".[127]

The Padre's answer makes us understand that if He, absolute Love, to whom everything is possible, when invoked

---

[126] Letters I, p 312.
[127] Rosetta Rappa, Natalino's daughter, Biella. 2.12.1999.

does not intervene, it means that for us good health could not always be a good thing, likewise illness and death could not always be a bad thing.

One day in church Enzo Bertani introduced P. Pio to two grieved and broken-hearted creatures: a mother and a father. Expressing their misery for the death of their young son, they complained about the "terrible punishment they had received from God".

The Padre, learning their trial, comforted them assuring the couple that their dear son was in Heaven. When the Saint went back into the friary , Enzo who was accompanying him, emphasized the great trial those two parents were being put through. But P. Pio added: "You have no idea of what the Lord has spared them from!"[128]

In another occasion the Padre always to Enzo, talking about painful circumstances, said: "We can see what happens to us but we can't see what the Lord spares us from".

To end the subject we report the following testimony. It could help us to understand the mystery we have spoken about.

"Who knows how she would have ended up"

Sister Vincenza Tremigliozzi recounts: "My sister Anna took a course to become a nurse in Naples, where she was much appreciated; so she decided to stay in that town to carry out her profession. But after two years P. Pio called her to San Giovanni Rotondo: the hospital Home for the relief of Suffering had just opened and the Padre wanted her with him. She was 22.

---

[128] Enzo Bertani, San Giovanni Rotondo 4.12.1995.

After a couple of years in the Gargano she became ill during the "Asian" flu epidemic; but she stayed in bed only a few days and then returned quickly to her job. She felt ill again and against the doctor's predictions she died.

All our family were filled with anguish and disoriented. Mum banged her head against the wall. I watched feeling devastated.

One morning, ten days after my sister's death, Sister Lucilla, a nun with me, at the end of confession heard the Padre ask her: "Where is Sister Vincenza?".

She answered that I was in the convent and the Saint said: "Tell her to come and see me".

I rushed to church and went in the confessional; he took my face between his hands and said: "Where do you think your sister is? We have sent her to Heaven!".

And after a brief pause he added, clearly saying the words: "Who knows how she would have ended up!".

With those words P. Pio opened a window on the mysterious plans that God has for us. I often repeated to myself "Who knows how my poor sister would have ended up if she had stayed in Naples".

Little by little a great peace settled in my heart".[129]

9. Bilocation

Bilocation is a paranormal phenomenon in which an individual is seen in two distinct places at the same moment of time. It has taken place in the lives of a lot of saints; we quote only two, St Francis of Assisi and St. Anthony of Padua.

---

[129] S. Vincenza Tremigliozzi, San Giovanni Rotondo, 4.3.2005.

It is a difficult thing to explain. Some people are of this opinion: as it is physically impossible that a body can be in two places at the same time, consequently the body of the Saint will only be really present in one place and apparently in another. Bilocation therefore should be an apparition, in which one sees the image of a person and also hears the voice and feels benefited by all.

We know for certain that as this phenomenon is supernatural it is a result of God's work.[130]

There was once a discussion amongst the brother friars at San Giovanni Rotondo about St. Anthony's bilocation, who even though he was living in Italy, found himself in Lisbon in court to defend his father's innocence. P. Pio was present during the discussion and a confrère commented that perhaps the privileged servants of God didn't even notice the phenomena whilst experiencing it.

Our Saint intervened and clarified: "Certainly they realise that they are here and somewhere else. They may not know if it is the body or soul that is moving, but they are well aware of what is happening and they know where they are going".[131]

A testimony from Fr. Alessio Parente, as well as confirming that during that during the phenomena of bilocation the Saint is conscious of what is happening around him, adds some particulars.

Our confrère recounts.

"One afternoon P. Pio said to me: "If you wish to have a breath of fresh air, come with me tonight".

---

[130] Cfr. *Dizionario di Mistica*, Ed. Libreria Vaticana, Città del Vaticano 1998, s. v.

[131] FR GERARDO DI FLUMERI, *"I carismi di Padre Pio"*, in *Padre Pio da Pietrelcina, Approdo…, 77.*

To tell the truth I didn't take much notice of this particular invitation. That evening, after putting him to bed, he called me saying he felt cold. I must state beforehand that P. Pio slept with just a sheet and a light plaid, as he couldn't stand heavy blankets.

I covered him with a blanket as he had asked and returned to my room, but after a while he called me again. "I'm cold", he said and his teeth were chattering.

He continued to feel uncomfortable and cold until I had literally loaded him with blankets. The Padre must have taken a trip in a very cold region".[132]

This episode should therefore certify that also the body of one of God's servants experiencing the phenomena of bilocation, can be involved.

From the Chronicle of the Friary of San Giovanni Rotodo reporter we learn that P. Pio spoke of the phenomena of bilocation, in which he was a protagonist, more than once. But he did so with the freedom of spirit belonging to saints, with surprising simplicity and naturalness.

Here are some examples.

"14th Dec. 1953.

In the refectory, as our Provincial Father, who had taken a "holy visit" to the Tuscany Capuchin friars in India and who had traveled by plane was present, we were speaking of the speed of airplanes and praising it.

And P. Pio jokingly said " It's always time that goes by. It goes and goes! When I leave, I take less than a minute".

---

[132] This is during the last years of P. Pio`s life, 1965-1968. Our confrère's testimony was given in San Giovanni Rotondo, 21.5.1993.

We all laughed joyfully at this clear and innocent allusion of the Padre at his frequent bilocations. He was a little confused by that joyful laughter; but the truth was already out". (f345)

"15th May 1954.

After lunch whilst accompanying P. Pio upstairs the friars spoke of the preparations for the canonization of Pio X. P. Pio said: "Fine Pio X. I think a great deal of him. He is the Pope of Peace, serenity with a great heart. He seems a good Neapolitan".

Fr. Tarcisio from Cervinara asked him "Father are we going to the canonization?".

"Yes" answered P. Pio.

" Are we going together?".

"You get yourself a ticket, I've already got mine" concluded P. Pio" (f.360)

"4th November 1954.

Mr. Paolo Candiano from Lecco, one of P. Pio's spiritual sons, who was very fond of him, had this brief but interesting conversation with the Padre.

"Father, I've been to Rome for the liturgical proclamation of the Regality of Our Lady, and after Rome I dropped in to visit you."

"Did you see me in St. Peters' Square?" asked P. Pio.

"No Father!", answered Mr Candiano.

"Worse for you, you haven't got eyes that know how to look!" exclaimed P. Pio. (f.383)

"26th September 1957.

The Capuchin Friars of San Giovanni Rotondo were invited to Amendola airport on November 4th for the yearly celebration of the Armed Forces. They had the chance to sit next to a pilot and fly over the Gargano.

Fr. Romolo Pennisi from San Marco in Lamis said they once spoke of this in front of P. Pio and because they said that it was certainly a sufferance for him to be always closed inside, without being able to go out, P. Pio added "Thank goodness that I sort myself out" and he smiled good naturedly. (f. 459)

Fr. Carmelo from Sessano, superior for six years at San Giovanni Rotondo friary, states he felt the Padre's presence whilst holding conferences with the tertiary Franciscans.

One day he asked P. Pio to confirm this. The Padre said: "Why, do you mind?".[133]

Bilocation: a charisma to comfort souls.

A testimony given by Fr. Agostino from S. Marco in Lamis clearly tells us that P. Pio used this charisma to comfort souls.

We are in the years of P. Pio's segregation (1931-1933) when he was suspended from all sacerdotal duties. Fr. Agostino every so often went up to San Giovanni Rotondo: stayed with him for a while, heard his confession and gave him comfort. During a visit made 2nd January 1932, he told him of his trip to Florence at the beginning of December to take part in the religious ceremony in which Giuseppina Villani on the 8th, Feast of the Immaculate Conception, took her vows to become Sister Beniamina Crocifissa.

The Saint was moved listening to the description of the event, as Giuseppina was a much loved and respected spiritual daughter.

---

[133] Fr Carmelo Durante, Larino (CB) Summer 1986.

But let us follow what Fr. Agostino writes.

"As in Florence a sister told me that, after communion, P. Pio had appeared to her, to comfort and bless her, I wanted to check up with him. I asked him: "Do you often also take trips as far as Florence?".

He looked at me smiling. I added: "A sister told me so. Is it true?".

"Yes, Father", he answered humbly.

This testimony as it continues is important because it lets one understand that these "trips" are not planned by the Saint but by the Lord.

The dialogue between the two continues and Fr. Agostino asks: "The sister told me that afterwards she begged you to go to Sister Beniamina too… and you answered: I "haven't the obedience". Is that true?"

And P. Pio confirms: "Yes Father".[134]

In Capuchin slang the *obedience* "means" the permission given to a friar by the superior to be allowed out of the friary.

Here are some statements from those who have received help and comfort from the Padre, in this prodigious way prepared by God's love for his children in need.

1. Carmela Frosina Leonardis, during one of my visits to the P. Pio Prayer Group of Comiso, told me:

"My seven and a half year old son who was ill with glandular leukemia was close to death. Whilst we were around him, me my husband, the doctor, other people, twelve in all, he said: "Kneel down and pray!".

---

[134] FR AGOSTINO FROM SAN MARCO IN LAMIS, Diario, edited by Fr Gerardo Di Flumeri, Ed. Padre Pio da Pietrelcina, San Giovanni Rotondo 1971, 62.

We all did so except for my husband.

The boy looked at him. "You too, dad", he whispered. And after a brief pause he said: "He's passing by… P. Pio is passing by…P. Pio is here". Soon after he died.

I had not heard about this holy friar, but I enquired about him and in 1958 I went to San Giovanni Rotondo with my husband who quickly confessed, whilst I had to wait my turn: I hoped to do so within 15 days and booked my couchette back to Sicily.

The days went by and I fearing that I would lose my train booking, I asked a woman who was ahead of me in the queue if she would change her ticket number for confession with mine. She did so, but not very happily.

I went to confess and P. Pio asked: "Why did you change number? You would have been confessed just the same". I was petrified and unable to speak.

The Padre realizing my embarrassment added: "I will help you". So I only answered his questions.

He gave me absolution and then asked: "Why have you come? To tell me that your son has died? He is in Paradise, he is an angel of Heaven, but you must always be his mummy".

I asked him: "Will I be able to have other children.?".

P. Pio answered: "You will have as many as you wish, but you will always do God's will".

When I got home and told the family all that had been said, nobody could give an explanation to the Padre's last phrase.

Soon afterwards I became pregnant; a baby girl was born who died after only 15 days. Once again I was expecting and I had another daughter I called Giovanna.

One day we had to leave. Before leaving we went to the doctors' who prescribed a medicine for her that she took. But during the journey she became ill and died in my arms on the train.

P. Pio had prepared me to accept from life what God allowed".[135]

2. Giuseppe Vitiello, born in Ponza 3.1.1928, in the Summer of 1952 recounts.

"I was a sailor on an oil tanker. One night in the middle of the Atlantic Ocean, on the fifth day of navigation, after sailing from Gibraltar, an extra-ordinary thing happened.

I was going through a difficult period. Each night as usual, before going to bed, I said my prayers and then examined my conscience. Once again I said to myself : " I haven't harmed anyone and yet I can't find peace. I can't find a girl to marry and settle down with".

I fell asleep, when suddenly I woke up feeling someone's presence in the cabin. I could clearly see before me in a glow of light, a character with a beard who said: "Come and see me".

I went back to sleep peacefully.

The day after, thinking about the vision I thought I had a sign of protection and comfort from the patron saint of Ponza, St. Silverio pope and martyr, whose tomb I usually prayed at when I went back to my home town.

At the end of the journey, I went back to Cagliari where my family had settled a long time ago, and I heard about P, Pio for the first time from Crespellari, the head of the Prayer Group who referred to the spirituality of the Capuchin friar. I remember this expression in particular: "P. Pio is a friar who confesses well".

I started thinking about going to San Giovanni Rotondo to talk to him about my situation. The occasion to go came up when

---

[135] Carmela Frosina Leonardis, Comiso (RG) 22.11.1996.

a cousin of mine got married at Mercogliano near Avellino: the day after the wedding I went to San Giovanni Rotondo.

I booked confession and after eight days had the good fortune to talk to the Saint. He examined my conscience and amongst other things asked me: "Did you ever steal?".

When I answered no, he said: "What about when the allies landed during the war. Didn't you do so then?".

I answered: "Father, it was a necessity!"

And he said severely: "It didn't belong to you!".

Then he added: "You don't go to Mass. When you come ashore you go to see your relations but you don't go to Mass".

He cleaned up all the stains I had on my conscience. For penance I had to say 15 Our Fathers, Hail Mary's and Glory be's for 15 days. Then I found a little peace.

I returned to San Giovanni Rotondo in 1954 and I confessed; even though I had the feeling that the mysterious person who had appeared to me was P. Pio, I did not ask him if it was so.

On my third meeting I spoke to him of the vision I had had in the Atlantic and I asked him: "Was it you?".

"Yes , it was me", he answered adding: "I called you to live your life well".

I started to be affected by the spiritual atmosphere you could breath in San Giovanni Rotondo. I asked to become a Franciscan tertiary and on 4th October 1959 I was dressed with the scapular by Fr. Giovanni Crisostomo Zarrella, in the inner chapel of the friary.

In the meantime I had met a girl in San Giovanni Rotondo. One day P. Pio said to me: "Get married, I will bless the marriage". And so he did. [136]

---

[136] Giuseppe Vitello, Cagliari 20.4.1999

3. Fr. Vittricio Mabellini, capuchin from the Religious province of Milan, offers us this testimony.

During the occupation of Milan, the German soldiers made a round up. They searched houses and captured men to deport them to Germany. Amongst them was a lieutenant of the Italian Army. As he was about to be loaded on a lorry, he saw a friar who took him by the hand and pulled him away shouting "Run, run!". He did so and was saved.

At the end of the war he often asked himself who the friar who saved him was.

One day together with some friends he went to San Giovanni Rotondo. As soon as he saw P. Pio he became pale and said to those with him: "He is the friar who saved my life!".[137]

4. Wanda Sellach states.

"My brother was a Prisoner of war in Africa during the second World war. One day my mother said to P. Pio:" Father, Pino will be on his own at Christmas. Go and visit him".

The Saint answered " I will".

After the holidays mum said: "Father, did you go to visit my son.?".

"I certainly did go."

"Did he see you?"

"As the blind man of Jericho heard Jesus pass by, so your son heard me pass by".

A few days later a letter from Pino arrived saying he had felt the presence of P. Pio in an "intensely strong way".[138]

[137] Fr. Vittricio. Mabellini, S.S. Annunziata Friary, Cogno, Summer 2000.
[138] Wanda Sellaci, San Giovanni Rotondo 7.12.1995.

5. Dr. Pietro Melillo tells us.

"My wife was expecting our fifth child, Francesco, and I asked P. Pio advice about what to do, if I should take her to hospital. "No", he replied , "she must give birth at home". I prepared a room at home in agreement with the midwife from the Home for the Relief of Suffering.

Every day I saw the Padre who asked me how the pregnancy was going: I felt very peaceful.

During the night of 7th August my wife started to feel labour pains, but due to "inertia uterine" the delivery started to become worrying, so much that I was tempted to take her to hospital for a caesarean section.

It was half past four in the morning, and before making a decision, I went on the balcony of the room where I could see the friary and mentally said to the Padre: "In a short while you will begin to celebrate Mass, whilst I do not know what to do".

A few minutes later the midwife from the room prepared for the birth told me my son was being born; I raced to join him, but I was struck by the noise of steps dragging along the corridor. I opened the door and saw the Padre's shoulder going down the stairs that lead to the floor below.

I was incredulous and went inside and saw the midwife with my son in her arms.

I went out of the room to follow P. Pio, but he had disappeared: looking at my watch I realized it was about five o'clock, the time the Padre began to celebrate holy Mass. Befuddled but happy I went back to my wife's room. All had gone in the best possible way.

In the middle of the morning, towards 10 o'clock, I went to the friary to thank P. Pio for his help, and most of all for having honored me with his "presence" which he told me I deserved because I had believed".[139]

---

[139] Testimony written by Piero Melillo.

6. We have another testimony from the same Dr. Melillo.

"One day, towards the end of 1957, I was at San Giovanni Rotondo for my week's work at the hospital. Whilst I was in the corridor of the friary accompanying P. Pio to his cell I spoke of the work I did at Milan and expressed my wish that he would bless my study. He promised me he would.

When I returned to Milan I went to my study, where I met the lady who kept all in order. She was very agitated and told me that a few days before, whilst checking all was in order., she noticed a strange print of a "hand" on the glass which covered my desk. She told me no one else had entered the room except her and that she had lost a lot of time to get rid of that handprint on the desk.

The day after she went back to the study and noted the well defined hand print was still there, clearly showing the finger tips. Amazed and irritated she said to cancel the mark she had had to rub a lot with various products, a lot of elbow grease until it finally disappeared.

I understood everything: P. Pio had kept his promise to bless his study, leaving an evident sign of his visit.

I was happy, even if a little deluded that I had not seen the handprint".[140]

P. Pio prepares the entrance to Heaven

Some testimonies show us the attention of the Padre towards the seriously ill, reached by him in an amazing way.

1. Umberto Stefani, writes. "My dad, Giuseppe, was very

---

[140] Ibid.

devoted to P. Pio, whom he had met in December 1952 when he had been to confession. In January 1961 my father was taken to the clinic " St. Zita " at Lucca. He was diagnosed with an incurable illness with little or no hope of recovery.

After a few months of unprecedented suffering, he asked me to go down to San Giovanni Rotondo, to speak with the Padre, so that with his prayers he could obtain from God a healthy recovery.

My family got on very well with Fr. Onorato Marcucci, and as in the month of September he called in our town, I spoke to him and fixed an appointment to go to the Gargano.

When I arrived there the good friar took me to the Saint's cell. I told him about my dad and his wish to be cured.

He listened to me in a fatherly way and promised he would pray. However after the conversation with the Padre, I had the feeling a cure for the sick man would not be forthcoming.

I returned to Lucca, and assured dad of the Saint's blessing and interest, which was manifested in a tangible way, beyond all imagination.

The days went by and 20th September 1961 the vigil of his death arrived. The morning of 21st September my mother went to the clinic early and was stopped by a nun, who was also a nurse and on duty. She asked her: "Madam, who is that friar that came out of your husband's room so early this morning?".

The poor woman did not know what to say. "Perhaps it's one of the chapel chaplains, who went by to see him," she answered.

"No, it wasn't one of them", the nun replied.

Mum rushed to reach the room, she found dad looking serene, without pain, feeling tranquil. She thought perhaps it was the effect of the drugs containing morphine, which were given to him when his suffering was at his peak. He nodded to my mum to come closer and said: "Do you know I've been with P. Pio all night; we prayed together... Let's hope he grants me my wish".

The sick man spent the day peacefully, although he worsened hour by hour until he passed away at 22.15.

Giuseppe Stefani hoped to the very end he could receive the grace of recovery. P. Pio introduced him into the reign of light and peace. And in what a way![141]

I have discovered that this was the grace the spiritual daughters asked the Saint: " Father, do you promise you will assist me when I am about to present myself to God?".

2. During a check up Vittorio Scaramuzzi was diagnosed with a malignant neoplasia. As time went by things worsened.

The sick man one night said to his wife Laura: "How I'd love to see Fr. Nazareno again!". This was a Capuchin friar who was a good friend of the couple.

His wife answered: "If no one tells him, how he can the father come to see us?".

The following morning about 6.30. Vittorio awoke his wife and said: "P. Pio has been here and told me Fr. Nazareno is coming".

Laura remained silent not wanting to contradict her husband. However, after half an hour she heard some one knock on the door. Their friar-friend arriving from Pontremoli. He had left at 4 am to get to Modena early and deal with things regarding the friary, and had passed by to say hello.

As soon as the friar entered, he realized he was expected and a little curious he asked for an explanation. They replied that his arrival had been announced by P. Pio. The friar re-

---

[141] Written testimony by Umberto Stefani, Lucca 29.12.2005.

mained silent for an instant, but not at all surprised by what Vittorio and Laura had said. Whilst giving this testimony he told us. "When I arrived, you could still smell the perfume left by P. Pio".

Fr. Nazareno confessed the sick man, asked him, a bank manager, some advice and left. After a few months, Vittorio died.[142]

See you soon in Heaven

The last bilocation of P. Pio that we know of, took place on the afternoon preceding his departure for Heaven; the Saint went to Genova to say hello to our confrère, Fr. Umile Bonzi who had injured himself whilst falling on 29th August 1968.

22nd September 1968, about 16:30 Sister Ludovica Maria Laguzzi went to take Fr. Umile a cup of tea. When she entered the room she smelt a strong perfume of flowers, which filled the air, not understanding why, she looked at the virtuous friar.

He said in a natural spontaneous way: "P. Pio came to say hello and give me his last goodbye."

The next day Fr. Umile had to go to the "Sorriso" to see to some things he was taken by car by Mother Antonietta. In town all were speaking of P. Pio's death, which they had heard on the news. So did the driver to our confrère, who showed no surprise at the news. He just said, "Now only God is left on earth."

Then opening his heart he spoke of the visit he had received the day before from P. Pio, adding: "He told me: See you soon

---

[142] Fr. Nazareno Caselli, capuchin friar. Sassuolo, (MO) 14.9.2003.

in Heaven." Fr. Umile left this earth 9th February 1969, a few months after the death of P. Pio.

The Padre knew his brother friar well. He had often come down from Liguria to San Giovanni Rotondo. The friary Chronicle notes a triduum preached by him in 1949 for the "Pope's celebration."[143] There was an excellent communion of spirit between the two confrères.

We know that after the war Fr. Umile was a promoter for an organization to assist needy and abandoned children. Its name was "Sorriso Francescano" (Franciscan Smile) (1945). With his encouragement and the help of the confrères and of generous benefactors, it spread over Liguria and other areas.

Our Saints, who loved "men of good heart" who alleviated people's suffering and pain, appreciated the charitable commitment with which his brother friar worked energetically for more than twenty years. Our Saint also made use of this organization. In fact, he sent children from San Giovanni Rotondo to, Fr. Umile so they could be cared for.

P. Pio who was tender hearted and grateful went to thank and say goodbye to him.[144]

---

[143] Chronicle. 3rd April 1949, F.252.

[144] We learnt about the circumstances of the bilocation from a telephone conversation with Fr. Renato Gastaldi, capuchin friar, who follows the diocesan process for the beatification and canonization of Fr. Umile. See also the "Messaggio di *Padre Umile* (supplement to "Il Padre Umile" n. 7, September 2001.

10. Dreams

Another way, in which P. Pio visits those who need help or a word of comfort, is through dreams. This could leave one rather perplexed; I was myself the first time I heard about it. The interpretation of dreams has always been a difficult thing to do.

The Holy Scriptures referring to dreams admonishes, *"Do not let them occupy your mind."* they admit however that they can be *"sent from on High."* (Sir 34-1-7)

God spoke in dreams revealing the future and his plans, to people in the Old Testament such as Jacob's son Joseph (Gen. 37-1-11) and Solomon (Kings. 3-5-15) In the New Testament God let's, Joseph the husband of Mary, know of his plans through a dream. (Mt. 1, 20: 2-13.19.22.

Dreams therefore can be a prophetic sign, a vehicle for the Holy Spirits words.

Once discussing this subject of dreams with some spiritual daughters, they mentioned Tonina Teglia, sister of Father Isidoro of Bologna, Capuchin Friar, saying she could have given me some clarification.

I went to see her and she stated: "Once I spoke of dreams to P. Pio: "Father, many people say you appear in dreams and give advice as if you were there in person. Is it true?".

The Saint clearly and simply, answered: "It is a gift given to me by the Lord".

The Padre confirmed he had this charisma in another circumstance, when he let it be understood that one could not always completely trust the dreamlike vision.

One girl called Anna who was part of the Schola Cantorum directed by Mary Pyle, the American, told P. Pio she had dreamt of him, and she asked him if he had really been near her that night speaking to her.

The Saint listened carefully and said: "Up till this point it is me; after that it's your imagination".[145]

Rosaria Balacco also has a useful testimony for us to read.

She says: "One night I dreamt I had asked P. Pio for some advice. He gave me a precise answer, which I remembered perfectly when I awoke in the morning. However, I started to wonder if it really had been him speaking to me.

As it was nearing my day to confess I said to myself: it is useless to rack my brains, I will just ask him.

After a few days, I confessed and asked the same question without referring to the dream.

He answered: "And what have I already told you!".[146]

Reading these pages, we have seen cases in which the Padre sends messages or gives comfort through dreams. We are giving a just few of the many testimonies of this phenomena, starting with this entertaining episode.

1. A married couple couldn't have children and began to turn to P. Pio, so he could intercede for them to the Lord.

One day the husband changed the photo of him and his wife on their wedding day with one of the Padre. The photo was in a beautiful silver frame in their bedroom. He wanted to keep P. Pio's image always in view. His wife took offence at this.

A little later, the young woman became pregnant and was extremely worried she would lose the child. One night not long before she was due to give birth, she had a dream. She was

---

[145] *Notes…*, San Giovanni Rotondo 18.8.1997.
[146] Rosaria Balacco, San Giovanni Rotondo, 3.4.1996.

in the Maternity Operating room and before the gynecologist came in, she saw a man with a beard dressed in a white coat stand in a corner of the room. Then she woke up.

A few days later, a baby boy was born and all went perfectly well with no problems.

After a few months, the happy mother started to plan a trip to San Giovanni Rotondo; she wanted to see if the friar of the Gargano resembled the person she had seen in her dream, and if so thank him. She spoke about her dream to everyone, it had become an obsession.

Her husband seeing how agitated she was, to calm her down, kept saying: "Don't worry, it was a dream, just a dream just a dream nothing else".

At last, they made the trip. When they arrived at San Giovanni Rotondo the couple took their place in the cloister where P. Pio would pass. When after a moment the Saint arrived, he stopped near the husband, looked at him kindly and patting his shoulder with his hand said in an ironic and amused tone. "So it was all a dream, was it?".[147]

2. Probo Vaccarini tells us: "It wasn't long since I had been to San Giovanni Rotondo and confessed to P. Pio, but after a few days back home, a problem came up and I needed his advice. I turned to him one night before going to sleep: "Listen Father, I need to talk to you to have your advice, but I can't come to San Giovanni Rotondo again. Help me!".

That night I dreamt I confessed to the Padre and he said to me: "About that problem do this and this", giving me precise indications. I woke up whilst saying the prayers he had given me for penance.

---

[147] Anna Baroni, Chiavari 8.12.1994.

The next day I did as P. Pio had said and things went well, turning out for the best".[148]

3. Ressia Rosmini Zanotti in 1954 was ill with diabetes, which has caused her foot to become gangrenous. She was taken to hospital and the doctors told her she needed to have it amputated.

Her daughter Elda Zanotti sent a telegram to San Giovanni Rotondo to asks P. Pio for help. The answer arrived assuring the Padre would pray for her.

In the meantime, to the doctors who were waiting to know if they had to operate or not, the patient said she would let them know.

During the night, she dreamt of a beautiful friar with a beard, who with his finger said "No". She awoke and found herself immersed in an extraordinary perfume. In the morning when the doctors did their rounds she told the head of the department she didn't want to be touched.

A little later the nun came to medicate the foot and when she removed the dressing she found it dry with no rotting.

The next day the head doctor looked at the woman and said: "Continue to pray as you have and thank God".

Ressia was cured. She left hospital and her foot never bothered her again.[149]

4. Rino Girolimetti recounts.

"I was looking for a job; although I was married, I did not have a steady job that guaranteed me a peaceful life.

---

[148] Probo Vaccarini, Rimini 14.5.1998.

[149] Lavinio Laura, close relative of the miraculously healed woman, Mongrando (BI) 2.12.1999.

One night at Castelfidardo, where I was living, I dreamt of P. Pio and I begged him to help me. He answered: "Pray".

I asked him something else and he answered again: "Pray". I added one more thing, and he for the third time said: "Pray".

I really did start to pray. However, six months had passed from that unusual visit of the Padre and I had had no sign of an answer to my prayers.

It was approaching Christmas 1959. My wife, who was a teacher and I decided to go to Senigallia to spend Christmas with my parents. We left on 23rd December.

On January 2nd during the night, I dreamt of P. Pio, who said to me: "Tomorrow morning go quickly to Castelfidardo!".

"Father, I'll go on January 6th in the evening, as the day after my wife will be back teaching at school.

"You have to go tomorrow morning, I said!", he shouted at me.

I was so shocked I woke up.

In the morning, I spoke to my wife and we decided to leave. When I arrived home, as I opened the door I saw a note on the floor. It said a telegram had arrived at the post office some days ago. I rushed there to collect it and read: "Please call at the manager's office. "Signed "Bank of…".

I went and spoke to the manager who said, "Mr. Girolimetti, you have finally come; if you hadn't come today we wouldn't have given you the job".

I got the job of collector and worked there until retirement.[150]

---

[150] Rino Girolimetti, San Giovanni Rotondo, 22-11-2004.

11. Perfume

Fr. Gerardo Di Flumeri observes: "We know that during their life and after their death, the bodies of some saints often emitted particular perfumes or sweet-smelling scent, as they call them in mysticism.

When St. Theresa of Avila died, the water with which her body was washed remained scented. The body of St. Domenico was found perfectly conserved and gave of a heavenly odour long after his death.

It is an extra-ordinary grace that God concedes to many holy souls.

Our Saint P. Pio was gifted with this grace. There are irrefutable testimonies of it: the number of people who affirm they have smelt a particular perfume on the things he touched, or even in the places, he passed through is countless. That perfume could also be perceived at a distance, speaking or even just thinking of him".[151]

The first to notice the perfume that the person of the Padre gave off were some spiritual daughters. When they mentioned it to him the Saint was surprised. Nina Campanile states this.

On a splendid day in January the 3rd or 4th of 1918, she went up to the friary together with her friend Girolama Longo, hoping to see the Padre. Entering in the cold, gelid church she started to meditate when she was assailed by an intense perfume of violets; she was amazed that in the middle of winter that could be possible because even if violets and wild flowers could be found outside the friary, it certainly was not the right Season for them to be flowering.

---

[151] FR GERARDO DI FLUMERI, *I carismi di Padre Pio, in Padre Pio. Approdo…*, 78-79.

She thought perhaps some woman wearing lots of perfume had entered before her.

Whilst she was pondering a thousand ideas, P. Pio came out of the sacristy; he did not disturb her prayer, but left a trail of rose perfume.

A few days before the Padre had held a conference for his spiritual daughters about poverty, and from Miss Campanile`s lips escaped the words: "Is it possible that the friars are now using refined soaps, those that keep their perfume for a long time?"

She could no longer remain absorbed in prayer and decided to go out just outside the church. There she heard happy laughing voices from other spiritual daughters. On seeing her they said: "What a perfume one smells as the Padre goes by. What a fragrance! You can smell it from afar!".

Then she confirming what the others asserted began to say what had just happened to her in church.

P. Pio was most embarrassed and tried to make Nina change subject, with many a nod, a wink or a nudge but she was unstoppable.

So the Saint exclaimed: "What are you saying? What perfume? Perhaps you smelt something stinky, seeing as I've eaten beans!". Roaring laughter followed.

Soon after the Padre left the good lucky daughters and went inside.

The day after Nina went to the friary for a spiritual discussion with P. Pio, who seriously and a little worried asked her: "Did you really smell perfume yesterday?".

"Yes, Father, certainly I did. Why can't you smell it?".

"No, no, and no again! I can assure you that I can't smell it", replied P. Pio.

Then he explained: "Listen these gifts are given by He to souls are not for their personal sanctification, but so that they may attract other souls to take to the Lord; gifts like the searching of one's heart, clairvoyance and prophetic spirit. All these things do not increase holy grace, but they are means to call other souls to God".[152]

Nina Campanile also tells us of the perfume emanated by all that P. Pio wore.

"Rosinella Gisolfi did P. Pio's washing and I took it to her. Every Thursday afternoon I had my spiritual meeting. The Padre came down into the guest rooms, where I was waiting and in a pillowcase, he brought me his washing. That laundry gave off an intense exceptional perfume. My hands remained impregnated with it".[153]

As well as the spiritual daughters, the first to speak of the perfume were our confrères, who from 1916 to 1932 spent time, in the friary at San Giovanni Rotondo to study and to take their first steps towards priesthood. We will quote only two.

Bro. Ludovico Rinaldi from San Giovanni Rotondo assured us that: "P. Pio left a trail of perfume as he went through the various rooms in the friary".[154]

And Fr. Federico Carozza states: "Sometimes to know where P. Pio was all you had to do was follow the trail of perfume".[155]

---

[152] Nina Campanile - testimony recorded on tape by Fr Gerardo Saldutto at San Giovanni Rotondo, 20. 3.1973.

[153] Ibid.

[154] Fr. Ludovico Rinaldi. San Giovanni Rotondo, 5-5-1993.

[155] Fr. Federico Carozza, Venafro (CB) June 1986

The meaning of the perfume

One day Fr Giambattista Colavita, who lived for several years with P. Pio, on hearing that people talked of the mysterious perfume they smelt in certain circumstances and attributed it to a message from the Padre, asked the Saint for an explanation.

The Padre said: "It is a sign that I am near to the soul."[156]

The Saint gave the same answer to Countess Telfener, who had asked him: "Father, some smell the scent of violets, others of roses or lily of the valley, and others of phenic acid. Is there a meaning for this difference?".

"It just indicates my presence", replied P. Pio [157]

Angela Borrini from Novara also wanted to know the message of the perfume attached to the various flowers: rose, violet, cyclamen…, and asked the Padre who answered ironically: "I haven't studied this as yet".[158]

The Saint however let it be known that, when the fragrance was not of flowers it could indicate a reprimand, but still a sign that he was near.

One day Rosa Cancellario asked him: "Father, what does the smell of phenic acid that I smelt mean".

"Pray, purify yourself and watch out for temptations. There is something wrong".[159]

---

[156] Fr. Giambattista Colavita, San Severo (FG) 2.2.1986.

[157] Rina Giostrelli in Telfener, San Giovanni Rotondo 6.5.1993.

[158] Notes…, San Giovanni Rotondo 19.5.1993.

[159] Ibid.

Perfume as approval

A Spiritual daughter states:

"I was in San Giovanni Rotondo in the Spring of 1965. I prayed for all the people who had ask me to pray for them. But every so often, a cousin of mine, who was living in sin with a fellow, came into my mind. I started to pray for her and I felt the desire to meet her, to make her understand that she was not following God's rules.

One day the Padre was on the balcony, In my heart I said to him: "Father, I would like to meet my cousin to let her see the error of her ways". I smelt a wave of perfume.

I continued: "I'd like to send her a postcard, but it is only an excuse to get closer to her when I return home". Once more perfume filled the air.

I continued: "I'll say I want to tell her about the marvelous things that happen at San Giovanni Rotondo". For the third time I was drowned in perfume.

I wrote the postcard and after a few days I left to return home.

After a few weeks, 22nd May, my cousin Rosa's birthday, I went to Bolzano: I wanted to help her get out of that situation. When I got to her house, I spoke to her about P. Pio and noticed that she was interested and listened carefully. She insisted that I stayed with her and I stayed for three days; also, because I wished to meet the man she was having an affair with. The third day he came. He was divorced, therefore the two could not be joined together in marriage.

When I returned home, I wrote to Rosa one letter after the other, storming her with messages.

After six months she went back home to her mother. After

a few years, she found a good young man, and started a family with him in accordance with God's laws".[160]

Comfort

Mr. Arrigo Rosazza Prin. (from Rosazza, Biella) confessed to P. Pio 9th Febuary 1961. He was a surveyor and during the summer months was part of the team of a building yard that high in the mountain, constructed hydroelectric plants. He only went down into the valley occasionally and when he did so, he did not worry about going to church. Therefore, he confessed this sin".

"How many times have you missed Mass?", asked the Saint.

"I don't remember exactly," replied the penitent.

"What's that, don't you remember how many times you've missed Mass?".

"No Father".

"I will not absolve you, go and confess to someone else", said the Saint ending the confession.

He stayed down in San Giovanni Rotondo, reflecting on the problems of his soul and after a few days confessed to one of the shrine priests, who listened and talked to him for a long time.

With his conscience clear, he took the way back. During the journey, he smelt a strong particular perfume, which accompanied him until he reached home.[161]

---

[160] Alma De Concini, Terzolas (TN) 23.7.1995.
[161] Arrigo Rosazza Prin, Biella 6.12.1999.

Warnings and protection

Teodoro Grossrubatcher from Selva di Valgardena tells us.
"In June 1972 I went to Mass and whilst there I smelt the Padre's perfume. Afterwards along with three sons, I went to the wood to bring some trunks of pine and larch to the valley. I loaded two on the sledge; they were about 4 meters long and fifty or sixty centimeters wide.

Whilst I was coming down, going through a patch of undergrowth, I put my foot on a twisted branch, which sprang up to chest height and blocked my way. The sledge hit me but it did not knock me over, just gave me a little push that pulled me out of the way and went on to crash into a tree.

When I realized what had happened I thought about that wave of perfume I was aware of during Mass: the Padre had informed me that he was near me".[162]

A similar thing happened to Piero Melillo.
Whist he was traveling by car and going rather fast, he smelt a wave of perfume. He remembered that one day he had asked the Padre the meaning of that phenomena and the Saint replied: "My son when you smell it, be careful".

Luckily, he slowed down, but not enough to avoid going off the road. He was lucky though: he was not hurt and the car was not badly damaged[163]

---

[162] Teodoro Grossrubatcher, Selva di Val Gardena (BZ) 25.11.1993.
[163] Written testimony by Piero Melillo.

IV. A FATHER'S HEART

After examining the rigour shown by P. Pio in wanting the penitents who turned to him to be enlightened in their spiritual journey, to observe God's rules, let us now look at his heart, which drew many souls who were hungry for light and comfort.

1. Soul companion

Those who had remained waiting quite a long time without absolution, when they received God's forgiveness through P. Pio, felt "reborn "to a new life.

"The countenance of these folk", writes Fr. Pellegrino-"became bright with the smile of regained peace, due to their happy meeting with P. Pio... The day of forgiveness, which took place in the little Capuchin church, became the happiest day of their life. The splendour of true free spirit, regained in the warmth of a severe but spirited confession, had in a second driven from their mind the horrible nightmares and the poisonous grip of wickedness and the muddy darkness of vice".[1]

The true joy they felt, fruit of the Spirit, became irrepressible and was shown by those lucky people to all those around

---

[1]   FR PELLEGRINO FUNICELLI, *L'intruso*, in *Voce di Padre Pio*, June 1981, 9.

them. It seemed as if the Holy Confessor took no part, apparently resting unperturbed.

Fr. Pellegrino, always ready to scrutinize the soul of his spiritual father, asked him some questions: he wanted to know how responsible or involved the man of God felt in the life of a soul, who after realizing and confessing his errors was converted. He said to him: "Father, I am convinced because of what I have heard from you, and for what I have noticed in you, at those moments, to see before me a confessor who does not end his action when he gives absolution".

P. Pio, always ready to oblige, answered using images that are most effective: "Yes, it is true; I accompany all my penitents as if I were their *shadow*".[2]

In addition, returning to the concluding act of confession, absolution, in which he put the penitent on the righteous path to the heavenly Father, the Saint added: "that is the exact moment that I feel my duty to be the souls "*companion*" .The duty entrusted to me by the Holy Virgin. To do this I have to find the way to escape from a prison without doors and windows. I would even be capable of escaping from paradise, until I could deliver these souls to Our Lady, with whom I made a pact".[3]

We must clarify two moments of the attention with which the Padre followed his children: the first is the ordinary care taken by a gardener who looks after his plants, making sure they lack nothing so they will grow, be strengthened and produce fruit; the second which can be defined charismatic takes place when the Holy Spirit enables this servant to go and help

---

[2]   Marian Month, day 21.

[3]   Ibid.

souls in a prodigious way, where distances, human conditions or otherwise count for nothing.

Simple Soul Care

The Padre, we know, affirmed in a categorical way: "My mission is to save souls". He lived for this end.

When on June 11th 1931, he was not allowed to go down into church and confess because the ecclesiastic authorities had denied him the permission to do so, he was broken hearted: he cried and suffered.

Fr. Raffaele D' Addario from Sant' Elia a Pianisi, head of fellowship, who gave him long awaited orders from Rome, states: "He lifted his eyes up to Heaven, and said: "Let God's will be done". Then he covered his eyes with his hands, bent his head and said no more. I tried to comfort him, but he only found consolation from Jesus hanging on the cross. Soon after (vespers) he returned to the choir and stayed till after midnight".[4]

To Fr. Agostino Daniele from San Marco in Lamis, his spiritual director, who also wished to console him saying: "All will come out for the glory of God and well being of souls". the Saint answered: "But it is for the souls that I feel the pain of this trial".[5]

He was allowed to take up his apostolate again two years later. P. Pio when confessing listened alternatively to people living at San Giovanni Rotondo and those from further a field.

[4]   Alessandro da Ripabottoni, Padre Pio da Pietrelcina. Ed. Centro Culturale Franescano, Foggia 1974, 321-322.
[5]   Fr. Agostino da San Marco in Lamis, Diario by Fr. Gerardo Di Flumeri, San Giovanni Rotondo 1971, 59-60.

The latter complained to the superior of the friary: "It is not fair that, a few have to share with many, half of the Padre's precious time."

Fr. Carmelo Durante, who took note of the comments and criticism of those who came to the Gargano, referred them to the Saint who answered: "My son, what they say means little. Look, those from out of town come every now and then; they confess and leave. I see them and confess them once or twice, a few times, that is all. Therefore I cannot follow or direct them spiritually.

The locals instead are here and can come and confess on fixed days. I can therefore direct them spiritually and improve their souls: they need this guide. Therefore it is necessary to use a particular turn for them. It is not, as they say, a question of preference, or privilege, without reason or for human reasons, but for their spiritual well-being that needs it. So let's continue to do as we have always done".[6]

The Padre followed his spiritual children with careful attention so that they stayed in grace and reached perfection, this is stated in a few testimonies.

Pietro Cugino, called by all *little blind Pietro*, one of the most well known people in San Giovanni Rotondo states: "P. Pio wanted me to confess every eight days. If I did not go, he would come looking for me.

One day I was helping the friar in the kitchen. He called me, taking me by the hand he led me to a corner of the cloister corridor where he heard my confession. In another similar occasion, I commented that I did not have much to say, and he replied: "Have you seen a housewife who has a beautiful piece

---

6   Fr. Carmelo Durante, Testimonianze, 1. 106-107.

of furniture? She dusts it every morning, because she always sees a speck of dust. We must do the same with our soul where there are always faults".

In these cases, he examined consciences; but he didn't just ask questions, he also added short comments on sins and virtues".[7]

In the zeal, he has for souls; P. Pio shows the nagging worry of which Paul speaks, writing to the Corinthians. "*My jealousy on your behalf is the jealousy of God himself; I have betrothed you to Christ, so that no other but he should claim you, his bride without spot*". (2. Cor.11, 2).

Our Saint wanted his spiritual children to go to confession weekly; he agreed to confession every ten days only because of the large number of people wishing to confess. He expected punctuality and respect of the appointed times.

"Once", said Enedina Mori, near to a holy day to which was bound a plenary indulgence, I confessed to a different priest. I feared I would have been unable to confess to the Padre within the eight days necessary to fulfill the indulgence.

When I went to his confessional again, after about two weeks, he leaned out a little and said: "You go over there, because you are not local".

"Father, it's me, Enedina; Father I am local!", I shouted.

He ironically said: "Oh you are not from out of town are you? You're local are you?".

Then he listened to me and said seriously: "Remember that I'm responsible for your soul".[8]

Piero Melillo tell us a similar episode.

---

[7]   Pietro Cugino, San Giovanni Rotondo, 7.9.2000.

8   E. Mori, San Giovanni Rotondo, May 1993.

He writes: "P. Pio was my confessor and as I went to San Giovanni Rotondo each month to operate at the Home for the Relief of Suffering, I confessed to him regularly.

In the spring of 1958, some friends of mine who heard me speaking of the Padre, but had never met him asked if they could come with me to the Gargano. We left Milan by car and had a good trip; naturally enough the conversation was about the Padre and the extra ordinary facts about him.

We arrived at the hotel in the evening and before retiring for the night, we planned to go the following morning to attend to the Mass celebrated by him at 5.45 am to meet him in the sacristy. However, none of us wished to meet him with our souls not "candid," so we decided to go early in the morning to a nearby friary to "purify" ourselves, and so we did.

At 10.00 am, after the woman's confession, before starting my work in the hospital, I went to the friary to say hello to the Padre. I met him in the corridor on the first floor. Usually when he saw me he gave me a hug; but that morning he moved away and looking deeply into my eyes, as only he knew how too he said: "Where were you this morning?".

I felt as if I was dying and stuttered some made up excuse. He turned his back upon me and accompanied by two brother friars went towards his cell. He opened the door and turning saw that I was following him. He looked at me again and said: "Where have you been this morning?".

I thought I would faint my knees went weak, I felt terrible both body and soul. After a second or two which seemed like a century, P. Pio realizing that I could no longer bear his gaze became gentler and closing the door said: "Remember not to do it again".[9]

---

[9]   Piero Melillo, written testimony.

Extra ordinary care

An example of how with a particular charisma the Holy Spirit enabled this zealous servant to follow his children when they were far away is given by Lucietta Pennelli.

She began to confess to P. Pio when she was six or seven. She became a little spiritual daughter among many others who were older and adults. To stay close to him she decided not to marry, and she was in union with him every day during prayer: in the morning she attended holy Mass and in the evening when he knelt before the tabernacle to greet Jesus and his Heavenly Mother, she was there.

She says: "During the period of segregation inflicted on the Padre, I had to confess to another priest. I believed all was going well in my soul because I was never reprimanded. When the Padre received permission to hear confession once more, he pointed out one by one the things that hadn't gone well in the two year period I hadn't been able to entrust my soul to him".[10]

The Saint was right when he assured his children, "I am near you night and day together with your Guardian Angel".[11]

1. Fr. Gian Battista Lo Monaco was very attached to P. Pio. By giving us his diary, he lets us see with what strength, in absolute naturalness, the Padre gave him, the assurance he was near him in his spiritual journey. Here are two examples.

4th March 1940 he was in the sacristy. Whilst the Padre took off his holy vestments after Mass he said: "P. Pio I feel you are always close to me. Is it on obsession or is it true?".

---

[10]   Lucietta Pennelli, San Giovanni Rotondo, 5.12.1995.
[11]   Notes…San Giovanni Rotondo, Maggio 1993.

And the Saint: "Is what an obsession?".

"Perhaps it's just a sensation I have", added Fr. Gian Battista. P. Pio: " What is the sensation? A little confused the priest asked; "So then it is true isn't it?".

The Padre, smiled and nodded yes it is.

23rd December 1965 Fr. Gian Battista was at San Giovanni Rotondo to spend some time with the Padre.

In a lucky moment he found himself alone with the Saint and said: "I often call you. Do you hear me Father?".

"Well I'm not deaf yet!" answered P. Pio.

The Padre always walked besides this son. Fr. Lo Monaco saw P. Pio for the first time in 1937. After his ordination as a priest 11th July he was given permission by his superiors to go to San Giovanni Rotondo to meet the Saint; however after a few days on the Gargano his lack of funds forced the young man to break his ... spiritual honeymoon. Whilst saying goodbye to the Padre he heard him say: "And why are you leaving?".

He was forced to tell him the reason why.

On hearing this, P. Pio pulled from his pocket some money destined for Masses and said: "Here you are, say some Masses for the intentions of those who have made Mass donations."

He stayed a few more days and then left but from that day the young priest, although he lived thousands of kilometers away from San Giovanni Rotondo never broke his relationship with his spiritual father.

Reading this excellent priest's notes we can see what an intimate spirituality the Padre established with his spiritual children.

In a conversation he had with the Saint on Tuesday 25th April 1939, Fr. Gian Battista spoke to the Padre of a doubt he had.

"Father, for quite a while every day in Mass I ask the Lord the gift of a painful participation in his sacrifice. May I continue to do so? Is it in agreement with Our Lord's wishes?".

"You may continue to do so" answered the Saint. "Asking is a good thing, but leave all to God's will. Many times the wish is more effective than the work.. My motto is: "no asking and no refusals."

After a day or two 28th April the feast day of St. John of the cross, he said to P. Pio after saying Mass: "Father, see that the Mass says I am right: The Communio says: "Happy are those that suffer on earth Christ's passion for they will enjoy Heaven with him."

The Saint taking him by the arm, replied: "You are in a hurry and want to anticipate the grace…the willing ones at the most flank it, they don't anticipate it…prepare instead your shoulders, yes your shoulders because the crosses will come… they will come…".

The next day 29th April, Fr. Gian Battista spoke to P. Pio: "Father, you look very tired and pale, you have been confessing for too long".

 Stroking his forehead the Padre answered, "I was tired before I began confessing. I had a terrible migraine this morning. But, he added smiling: "Let the Lord's will be done"

"P. Pio, how I envy your tiredness!", exclaimed the young priest.

"There will come a time when you call me to help you". The lucky questioner continued: "I feel confident in my heart that the Lord will satisfy me. What do you think? In your words "prepare your shoulders", I see an answer from Jesus."

The Padre: "Well then prepare your shoulders and pray a lot, doing so you'll face all like a lion".

In the afternoon, after reciting the breviary in chorus, in the corridor the young man asked: "P. Pio why did you say to me this morning "a time will come when you will call me to help you ? I call you and my Guardian angel to help me every day"".

And, the Saint: "My son, you ask for sufferance, you ask for pain, for work and… When these come you will exclaim: "I can't go on, I can't stand it!".

" Well then don't leave me on my own", replied the young man, "stay always, especially then, by my side". Help me to prepare my shoulders".

"Very well, very well." concluded P. Pio. Two of us will suffer."

The following morning Sunday 30th April the Padre confirmed his promise. Fr. Gian Battista had said he would celebrate Mass for himself and P. Pio, adding: "Father, don't you think it is beautiful both of us suffering in the same chalice?".

The Padre gazing in to his eyes, with a smile said "yes". Then he put his hand on the boy's shoulder, thanked him and added: "I will do the same. I will say a Mass for you. I will always be with you. Vae soli! (Trouble strikes the man alone). We will suffer together. Don't worry".

Fr. Lo Monaco was reassured of how the Padre would keep his promise, when he reminded him to remember the seminarists of Catania in Holy Mass. P. Pio replied: "Very well. I always keep my promise. What ever I start I finish. When I can't say mass I know how to make up for it".[12]

2. One of his dearest closest spiritual daughters, Giovan-

---

[12]   Testimony written by Fr. Gian Lo Monaco.

na Rizzani, Marquis Boschi, experienced the Padre's vigilant continuous presence while she was in Naples, but through the hard manners he was not afraid of using in confession.

Although she was an extremely scrupulous woman, she had the bad habit of repeating the sins of her past life. The Padre was not in favour of this and begged her not to do it again. Once whilst confessing at San Giovanni Rotondo, having hinted once more at a sin she already confessed, P. Pio in a severe tone said: "Look here, the next time you do it, you'll get a sharp slap".

She, who had always seen the gentle side of P. Pio thought he was joking.

One day she went into church near her villa at Marechiaro and asked Father Cattaneo to hear her confession. She fell back into her old habit of repeating sins already confessed. After receiving absolution, she moved near the altar to receive communion. Whilst she was ending her penance, the sound of a loud slap echoed all over the church. It was so loud that the priest who was still in the confessional came out to see what had happened.

Then she remembered what P. Pio had promised to do if she disobeyed.[13]

3. We know that the world famous tenor Beniamino Gigli was so attached to P. Pio he felt the need to often come to San Giovanni Rotondo. A note in the Chronicle tells us how P. Pio followed this son of his.

We read: "On December 1st last year in the father provincial's room, Bro. Daniele Natale from San Giovanni Rotondo

[13] Testimony by Giovanna Rizzani, Marquis Boschi recorded by Pasquale Bellardini 28-6-1989.

asked: "May I say something?" P. Pio was there. Daniele continued: "The radio said that Gigli when he was dying said that P. Pio was beside him to help him." And P. Pio lowered his eyes.

Bro. Daniele continued: "Gigli used to say: "When I am abroad, P. Pio is always beside him. When I am in Italy, I no longer feel him". P. Pio commented," Here we are at home".[14]

4. Extremely enlightening is the testimony given to us by Carmela Marocchino.

She had come from Canosa to San Giovanni Rotondo where she stayed a few days, enjoying being near to the Padre, whom she already knew.

On the morning of her return home, she went to confess and say goodbye to the Saint. She heard him say: "All the best to your dad, and tell your sister to sort herself out. As for you be strong, prudent and wise in the difficult way ahead".

Carmela rather surprised said: "Father so you are near me aren't you?".

And P. Pio: "If I wasn't near you, how could I see how you live at home?".[15]

The Padre showed Dr. Piero Melillo that he was able to follow his every move. This was certainly a gift from God.

The doctor tells us that one day he was having a discussion in front of the little church belonging to the friary. They were talking about how one of the ecclesiastic worked. This was reported to the Padre and perhaps Piero was blamed for something he had not said or done.

---

[14]   Chronicle..., f. 493: 25th February 1958.
[15]   Carmela Marocchino, San Giovanni Rotondo 17.9.1985.

After the women's confession when the Saint was returning to the friary, he saw the doctor. The corridor was crowded with people asking for prayers or to kiss his hand. On seeing the doctor P. Pio rebuked him sternly. Probably because P. Pio was so jealous of the Church's honour he wished his spiritual children to respect fully the Church institutions. To be most prudent when speaking of the Church, or those involved in ecclesiastical roles.

The poor fellow, who was used to the Padre's sweeter side, felt shattered.

Let us hear what he has to say.

"Those words wounded me more than a stabbing. I went down the stairs and out of the friary feeling bitter. I intended to leave San Giovanni Rotondo immediately and never go back. In the evening the hospital chaplain, a dear friend of mine came looking for me. He wished me to return to P. Pio and he forced me to go to the friary with him. We met the Padre in his cell where he had retired for the night. I knelt down and kissed his hand, rather distantly.

P. Pio looked at me and said: "I waited for you at 12.30pm (refectory time) and I didn't see you. I waited at 14.30 (the time of the men's confession), and you did not turn up then or before or after the afternoon religious functions You didn't even come before I retired to my room. What do you think you are doing?".

I answered that I intended to leave for Milan. He added: "What do you think, that I won't be able to come and get you half way?".

The Padre hugged him and his anger cooled down. The next morning the Saint made peace by an exquisite gesture. He offered the doctor a bunch of violets.[16]

---

[16] Piero Melillo, written testimony

The Padre's solidarity with his children

We find in Friary Chronicle a brief but significant story. "Young Viviana Guidi, blessed by P. Pio, turned to him because she was troubled by the devil in many ways. And Padre Pio: "Daughter, don't worry, I'll see to that fellow, the demon, for you".[17]

P. Pio had these reassuring phrases, like the one we have just read. For example to a man who had inner problems of homosexuality, and kneeling at the Padre's feet in confession confided his dramatic intimate suffering asking for prayers, the Padre answered: "I'll see to it".[18]

The Padre, speaking in this way, wanted his children to know that he was near them. He wished them to feel the warmth of his affection and assistance in daily life. To be certain of his help not only for their religious needs. He desired that they felt him morally united and supportive, ready to let them unload their problems on him.

All this to make them braver and surer: they who under his guide, regenerated in the Lord, took the road to perfection.

Let us look at other cases.

Here is a father, awaiting you

We know that P. Pio indicated the way of his cross to his spiritual children. He did not leave them alone on the long painful road.

---

[17] *Chronicle...*f.3837th November 1954.
[18] Testimony by the man who benefited from the Padre; Biella. 4.12.1999.

Maria Merla tells us: "Dad was seriously ill close to death. Mum was eight months pregnant and I was two years old. She felt on the edge of a deep pit.

The evening of October 14th 1935 she, feeling desperate, headed towards the friary. It was already late and evening shadows had started to fall. The path to the Capuchin friary was dark and she tripped and fell twice; but when she arrived at the church square she saw the friary door was still open. She was heartened.

She went in and saw to her amazement that P. Pio was waiting for her at the back of the little corridor. The poor woman kissed his hand and heard him say: "What have you come here for at this time of night?".

" Padre Pio, my husband is dying".

The Saint after a few minutes thoughtful silence answered: "Wait for me", and went into the sacristy.

He came out after a while, carrying a Crucifix about sixty centimeters long. "My daughter, this is the cross you will have to carry all your life. Remember that here is a father who cares for you and will wait for you", he said.

The next day October 15th dad died.

Mum went into herself, she became so depressed she wanted to commit suicide. She attempted it. She wanted to throw herself down a well that was near the house. As she was on her way there she heard a voice saying: "What are you doing? What are you doing? Killing yourself and the baby? And this one (referring to me), who will you leave her to?".

It was the Padre who was calling her. She listened to him and was bound forever afterwards to him.

My little brother was born and mum said to herself: "This boy must study!". So she began to bake bread which she then sold.

The Padre was happy and followed her every move., but when he saw that the job she had chosen was destroying her because she didn't rest enough, he advised her to take a job working for the Vasciaveo family from Cerignola. She lost a little independence but had a calmer life.

What mum was unhappy about was the fact that after listening to early morning Mass, she couldn't go up to the friary later on to take communion, when the Padre having finished listening to the woman's confession, distributed it. The ladies she worked for didn't give her the permission to go.

She complained of this to the Saint, who reassured her: "You come the same".

From that day onwards no one commented about her brief absences: the Padre had spoken to those he had to.

In this way P. Pio kept mum always near him, protected by his fatherly gaze.[19]

And what am I here for?

Maria who gave us the previous testimony has something else to say.

After she had received her diploma as a primary school teacher, she noticed a boy was paying her some attention. He wanted her to be his fiancé.

Before giving him her answer she wanted to speak P. Pio. Who, after remaining quiet for a while said: "You must not get married. Marriage is not for you".

The girl did not accept the Padre's advice immediately and every so often in confession brought the subject up but every

---

[19]   Maria Merla, San Giovanni Rotondo 15.04.2005.

time she did the Saint turned his face away.

One evening she went back to the friary to take part in the Eucharistic function celebrated by the Saint; and whilst he blessed all she said to herself: " Lord, if that young man is not for me, remove him from my heart and mind ".

Soon afterwards at home she realized her feelings for the boy had diminished. After a few days they disappeared completely.

Maria was given a teaching position at Motta Montecorvino (FG); Being far away from home she started to grow sad. One day after confessing to P. Pio she said: "Father, I feel lonely, I haven't got anybody!".

The Saint replied: " Do you believe in God?" and quickly added: "And what am I here for?".

Maria assures us that for the rest of her life she no longer felt the need to have a family: she felt the Padre close by.

Especially after his death, when she faced any difficulties she seemed to hear his voice saying: "And what am I here for?".[20]

Close to the heart

Gina Deiana at the end of her first confession with the Padre heard him say to her: "You will suffer a lot but I will always be close to your heart".

She thought the Saint said this, because as her fiancé had left her she was at her wits end. Then she realized the Saint was talking about her life in general during which she always really felt him by her side.

---

[20] Maria Merla, San Giovanni Rotondo 15.04.2005.

It is enough to think of the terrible moment when she was terrified of losing her sight. Glaucoma was diagnosed in both her eyes.

She assures us, she turned to P. Pio only and was cured. [21]

Spiritual Director... from afar

We know that P. Pio advised his spiritual children to find a confessor in their own towns, one they could see regularly to be sure to stay on the righteous path.

Fr. Pellegrino writes: "The Padre, although being the only person who had the right to direct his spiritual children, saved for eternity at the price of blood, didn't want to have the responsibility of personally leading the newcomers. It seemed as though he completed his task in shaking them and in confessing them.

One day, in the orchard, after listening to a conversation between a new convert and me, P. Pio intervened and said "But what are you getting up to? Let this poor fellow go and talk to his priest when he gets home. Do not confuse him. The church has wide arms. If we believe we can substitute those arms, we just cause confusion".

He believed the figure of the Spiritual Padre and confessor was irreplaceable. To many of his children he repeated: "Listen to your confessor's opinion. If you haven't got a confessor find one". [22]

Probo Vaccarini also received this advice from the Saint.

He followed it and was satisfied with the guidance and ad-

---

[21] Gina Deiana, San Giovanni Rotondo 3.12.2004.

[22] Fr. Pellegrino Funicelli, L'intruso, in Voce di P.Pio. June 1981, 9.

vice given by the spiritual father he had chosen. But one day when he went to church, he heard the bad news that this priest had been transferred.

Going to San Giovanni Rotondo he spoke, feeling disappointed to P. Pio, who said reassuringly: "There's me isn't there?"

"But you are here! What about when I'm at home?".

And P. Pio: " There is me... there is me! Do you understand?".[23]

The Padre is always near

After Alma De Concinis, a spiritual daughter from Trento, obtained from the Padre the promise he would have sustained her in her commitment to God, she felt the Saint's presence, experiencing all the comfort of this.

She was not married, but being part of a large family, eight brothers and sisters, she always had a thousand things to do and had to be at every ones disposal.

She confides: "In a moment of dejection and tiredness, whilst I was doing the washing, I heard: "Alma, Alma!". It was the Padre's voice. I heard it distinctly. It lifted me from the weight that was causing me anguish".

As time went by, it was 1960, seeing that the others were settled by finding a job or making a family she started to worry about her future. She had to make a decision and needed to talk to the Padre. She needed permission from others and money to do so.

---

[23] Probo Vaccarini, S Martino in Venti. Rimini 14.5.1998. See also Probo Vaccarini, Colloqui con Padre Pio, Ed. Casa Sollievo della Sofferenza, 1996,30. 1996-30.

One day whist in Predazzo (TN) with one of her sisters, she was preparing a meal. Moving a plate, she found 10.000 lire and she was tempted to take the money and run to San Giovanni Rotondo to speak to P. Pio. "But he", says Alma, "didn't want me to do so. So he came to me instead".

About 4 am, the next morning, whilst she was crying she saw the Padre come into the room. He went to the bedside and gave her his hand to kiss. Then he said: "Up to now you have helped everyone, now it's time to think a bit of yourself. Sort yourself out! Do you understand? Sort yourself out, get yourself a position".

Almost to check that what she had heard was really the voice of the Padre, she wrote to Wanda Sellach at San Giovanni Rotondo: " Have a word with P. Pio about me".

After a few days, she received a letter, which read: "The Padre said he is always close to you".[24]

I will always follow you

Maria Tremigliozzi was called by the Padre through a dream. She saw P. Pio who said: " Come and meet me".

"But I don't know how to come. I don't know the way", she answered and P. Pio indicated where to get the train and where to go.

Accompanied by her mother she arrived at San Giovanni Rotondo 2nd August 1942 and after a few days confessed, but when the Padre heard she did not go to Mass, he refused her absolution and sent her away.

The girl had a crisis. She stopped eating and sleeping and

[24]   Alma De Concini, Terzolas (TN) 23.7.1995.

did not want to see her fiancé, an air force lieutenant. Her mother was worried. She wanted to take her back to P. Pio. Only he could give her peace of mind.

After ten days, the two women were at San Giovanni Rotondo once more. The young girl trembling started her confession, but she was so emotional she could not speak.

"And now what do you want to say?, asked P. Pio with the kindness and good spirit of a mother. She did not answer, she seemed frozen.

The Padre continued: "Well, what do you have to tell me?".

"Father, I want to become a nun".

This is God's will, answered the Saint. Then asked: " But do you wish for an active life or closure?".

"I want to be a Franciscan, to be near you".

"But there are no Franciscans sisters here", added P. Pio. He continued: "For now you must answer God's call. Be assured however that the doors here will always be open for you. I will follow you wherever you may go".

The girl retuned home feeling much calmer. After a few months, she left to become a novice of the Pious Workers of St Joseph. She took the veil with the name of Sister Vicenza.

Whilst she was at Castel del Rio (BO) in the autumn of 1943, the zone suffered continual bombing during the war. She however felt that P. Pio was close to her.

On October 27th 1942, the town was violently attacked. The following night Sister Vincenza dreamt the nun's house was hit. She saw the attic fall on top of her, she closed her eyes and called P. Pio as dust and mortar enveloped her. She felt someone's chest leaning on her, protecting her face and letting her breathe. She was pulled unharmed from the rubble.

She woke up and told the Mother Superior all. The nuns left

and went to a safer zone. After a few nights, their house was literally destroyed by bombs.

Sister Vincenza was more than ever sure that the Saint followed her everywhere.

After taking her vows, she came to see P. Pio whenever she could. She expressed her wish to live close to him. Once P. Pio said: "They will open one of your houses here and later you will come too".

In 1952, the Sisters of St. Joseph opened a hostel called "the little convent". For the inauguration, the General Mother called Sister Vincenza and took her along. P. Pio went down from the friary to bless the new hostel and at the end of the blessing said to Sister Vincenza: "Are you happy now?".

 Then seeing that his spiritual daughter was not completely satisfied added: " Soon you will come here".

A few months later, without anyone moving a finger or saying a word to make her dream come true, Sister Vincenza was given by the Mother Superior the task of running the new hostel. Each time she feared she would be moved away from her spiritual father, the Saint said: "You will only leave here if I want you to."

Today more than 30 years after the Padre's death, Sister Vincenza is still at San Giovanni Rotondo.[25]

I always think about you

Mario Cappetta tells us.

"As I had to leave to go to a fair in Germany, to look at some Printing machines, I went to San Giovanni Rotondo to

---

[25]   Sister Vincenza Tremigliozzi, S. Giovanni Rotondo 16.5.1999; 25 April 2004.

ask P. Pio for his blessing. It was a Wednesday so I anticipated by two days the regular visit I made him every Friday.

I was away for two weeks. The following Friday when I returned I went up to San Giovanni Rotondo to thank the Padre for his assistance. I met him in the corridor, kissed his hand and gave him thanks. Fr, Eusebio who was with him, said as soon as he saw me: "We haven't seen you for fifteen days!". And the Padre: "No he's been missing for 17 days!".

The friars went into room number 5 and I, counting the days I'd been away, realized with wonder and joy that I really had been away from the Padre the amount he said.

So I knocked on the door and asked to enter to express my gratitude for the fatherly care and attention he showed me. The Padre said: "I always think about you".[26]

The Padre does not leave his children alone in danger

On the evening of 28th July 1995, the architect Giuseppe Gentile who was building the new church at San Giovanni Rotondo, went to say hello to P. Pio, before he went to bed. "Father, he said to him, "I have to go to Boiano, because tomorrow I have a case in court. My father-in-law assigned a house to my first wife, but now wishes to annul the act because she has died. I cannot accept this because I have a son who should have his mother's inheritance".

"You are thinking about the outcome of the case?... He'll shoot you!" replied P. Pio.

"Father, do you think I'm a sparrow?", answered the architect.

---

[26]   Mario Cappetta, Campitello Matese (CB) 21 August 1994.

And the Padre " Be careful, he is not joking".

"I'll do my best to be on guard"

The Saint blessed him and Geppino left. He arrived home about eight o'clock. Then next day he went to see his father-in-law to propose an agreement. He found him unshakeable and tough. "I still have a son and I must think of him, not my grandson", he said.

The case was taken to court and won by the architect. After the sentence, he stayed for a while in the courtroom refusing the invitation of relatives to have lunch with them. He excused himself saying: "I want to end the case and return to P. Pio."

His father-in-law who was furious, as he climbed the stairs shouted: "You have won the case, but I won't let you read the posted sentence in public!".

As soon as the architect was in the street his opponent, who was waiting armed with a revolver, ran up to him and put his insane plan in action. It was 13.00 and the first shot hit Geppino in the shoulder. He started to stumble but by his zigzagging, the next three shots missed their target.

He took refuge in a butcher's and fell on the floor. He would have died if the butcher had not immobilized the crazy pursuer.

He was taken to hospital and had an operation but the doctors were unable to find the bullet, which had struck him.

The wounded man kept repeating: "Get me my wallet, P. Pio's crucifix is in it". On the day the Padre gave it to him he said: "When you need me kiss this and I will be near you".

His wife Nina was told what had happened and she asked: "Is he dead?".

When she heard that he was in hospital she added: "Well then P. Pio will save him." She rushed to him full of hope.

She found two priests at his bedside comforting him. She

said: "Have you seen your father in law achieved his purpose?"

"Let the Padre know", said Geppino.

Her cousin sent a telegram to San Giovanni Rotondo.

The Saint was in the choir praying. When he read the telegram he said: "Just as I expected".

The evening came and then nightime. The architect couldn't find peace. "Who will cure me?", he cried to himself.

Towards midnight, he had difficulty in breathing, he looked towards the window and heard a rustling. The room was filled with a wave of perfume. The Padre had come. The sick man however did not improve, until eight days later in theatre when they managed to extract the bullet. P. Pio the evening of the new operation said to the friars in his room, who helped to put him to bed, "At last... this shoulder! I couldn't stand it anymore."

Bit by bit the architect regained strength and left hospital. Of the incident most of all he remembered the first terrible moments and said: "The hand that pulled me here and there, making the bullets miss me, did it belong to P. Pio or to the Guardian Angel he sent me?".[27]

A few days after the attack, on August 1st the father superior of the friary and I went to P. Pio's room. He was already in bed. Fr. Carmelo Durante from Sessano reassured him the patient was all right, and said: " I'm telling you this Father so you won't have another bad night worrying about him." And the Saint, referring to the previous nights, added with a smile: "Not only worrying about him".[28]

---

[27] Nina Campanella, widow of Gentile, Boiano (CB) 21.7.1997.

[28] Personal Diary.

Those who did not disappoint the Padre's expectations and tried to follow his teachings by being, as he said, "good Christians", felt his constant beneficial presence.

They could be certain of this. He was in the habit of saying: "I keep my promises".

One day Rina Giostrelli, expressed her fear that she would lose his protection. P. Pio jokingly said, showing her his hand: "Do you think you can escape from these claws?"[29]

2. The Good Samaritan

The evening of September 9th 1965, Fr. Onorato Marcucci and I put P. Pio to bed. He was very tired after working all day long, despite his age and his sufferings. However, he found it hard to go to sleep. Every so often, he asked us to change his position. "Turn me over please, on my other side", he repeated up to almost midnight.

Then Fr. Onorato came close to his bed and said: "Father, you certainly must have some thoughts on your mind that won't let you sleep". And he: "Thoughts! The troubles of humanity these are the thoughts for all".[30]

If it is true that the Saint acting as God's minister aimed first of all at the soul's well being, however in getting close to a person, he always looked at their whole being. He considered their needs, worries and sadness.

In the first chapter we have noted how the Padre in the confessional, showed himself to also be a doctor of the body.

We wish now to add some notes to show how much P.

---

[29]   Rina Giostrelli. San Giovanni Rotondo 7.01.2005.
[30]   Personal Diary.

Pio took an interest in the suffering, which marked penitents' lives.

The troubles of mankind at P. Pio's confessional

1. In the spring of 1967. Mrs Felicia Ulisse went to San Giovanni Rotondo to have a word of comfort from P. Pio: a year before she had lost a nine-year-old son, Francuccio. Whilst the surgeon was operating him to take out his tonsils out, by mistake he sharply cut the boy's aorta; he died immediately from loss of blood.

Neither she nor her husband Amerigo felt like filing a complain against the doctor, as they did not want others to suffer because of this accident. They were good Christians and decided to take from God's hands all he allowed in their life.

Although they enjoyed the company of another elder son, the sufferance they felt for the loss of the younger boy grew. To it was added the sadness that they could not have another child to bring happiness to their family.

When Felicia went to confession and began her conversation with P. Pio, she was so taken with the gentleness of the Saints words that she forgot her misfortune. After she had listened to his advice and received absolution she was about to leave the confessional when the Padre asked: "What about the loss of Francuccio, aren't you going to say anything? Nothing about all that has happened to you?".

That mother who felt she was living a heavenly moment, was brought back to harsh reality, but before she could say a word, the Padre said. "Don't worry, in a year's time you will have Francuccio again".

She retuned comforted to San Benedetto del Tronto and after a few months became pregnant. At the end of the year, as the Saint predicted she had a baby, who looked like her lost son. They gave the baby the son's name.

Sister Silvia Zoccari, who gave us this testimony ends: "This is the incredible story of those who put their faith in God.

It is true though as can verify, the dead boy's family". [31]

2. Mrs Maria Vezzoni tells us.

"I came to San Giovanni Rotondo in the spring of 1965. To be exact in the month of May, because my son was in the sanatorium, as he was suffering with tuberculosis. We could not wait to take him home. Meanwhile the doctors kept him in and were very vague when speaking of how his illness was going.

So I decided to turn to P. Pio.

I booked to see him but when my turn arrived, the friar who took charge of those going to confession, said: "Madam, P. Pio will not confess you because your dress is too short". I whilst waiting tried to avoid his gaze opened my zip, put a pin in my skirt and tried to pull it down. It hardly moved an inch.

As soon as the Padre opened the grate, before starting the confession , said: " Next time come with a longer dress."

I with tears in my eyes, after confessing spoke of my son. He said " My daughter, go home and don't worry. Your son is fine and will go home before you".

Since I continued crying he added gently: "Come on don't be foolish, your son has been cured".

As soon as confession was over, I rushed out of church looking for a telephone, to tell my son what P. Pio had said. As soon as I heard his voice, I burst into tears and could hardly speak.

He said: "Mum, don't worry, if you don't catch the train

---

[31]   Sister Silvia Zoccari, Porto Azzurro, Isola D'Elba, 17.4.2003.

quickly, I'll be home before you". I was surprised; He had said exactly what the Saint did.

As soon as I arrived in Milan, I went straight to the sanatorium to speak to the doctors. The doctor came towards me and said: "Madam, I have good news for you, your son is cured".

After a few days he was back home with family.

In this episode, we do not know what to admire most; the charity and gentleness of the Padre or his spirit of prophecy and clairvoyance.[32]

3. Luciano Livellara's mother needed an operation. The doctors delayed doing it because the patient had frequent changes of blood pressure. This affectionate son came down from Trieste to San Giovanni Rotondo and after confessing, he talked of this problem to the Padre, and asked his advice.

The Saint listened and looked at him intently. Then he added: "Do you love your mother?".

"Of course, Father", answered Luciano, a little surprised at his question.

The Padre smiled and then said: "Do not worry, no, no! Blood pressure indeed! Tell the doctors to operate without fear".

Livellara returned home. His mother's blood pressure went back to normal, she had the operation and all went well.[33]

4. Italo Mirco tells us.

"After receiving my call up for the army at the end of April 1953, 3rd May 1953 I reached Cuneo to begin my training for C.A.R. but I was very worried because I had left my sick mother at home.

[32] Maria Vezzoni, widow Casnaghi, San Giovanni Rotondo 26.9.1994.
[33] Luciano Livellara, Chiavari. 6-12-1994.

After giving birth to twins her stomach had lowered. At the least force, working at home or in the fields she felt ill. She was obliged to stay in bed. She was sick, lost consciousness and was unable to eat for three or four days. The various medical cures she tried had no effect. My mother's health had been a worry for me since childhood.

During a leave, I went up to San Giovanni Rotondo and stayed at a hotel. I already knew the Padre and I must admit at the vigil of every meeting with him I was always agitated. That night however after saying my prayers, I went to sleep peacefully.

Early in the morning, I went to his Mass and soon after confessed. He was sitting at my side and I felt his fatherly presence. I told him about my worries about my mum, Cristina Tomizzi.

P. Pio listened to me carefully said a few words then he gave me absolution.

From that day, my mother felt better and had no more pain for the rest of her life.

She died serenely on September 18th 1979. She was 84".[34]

5. A young contractor from Romagna bought a huge plot of building land. It was during the building boom and he wanted to make a speculation. Of course, to buy such a large area he was forced to ask the banks for a loan.

Unfortunately, for him, after a few months, the building market halted. He found himself in trouble with high interest to pay.

He felt lost and desperate. He turned to Fr. Guglielmo Gattani, capuchin friar and asked him to go with him to San Giovanni Rotondo and arrange a meeting with P. Pio. There was

---

[34] Italo Mirco, Campitello Matese (CB) Summer 2002.

however a big problem. Capuchin friars were not allowed to go to San Giovanni Rotondo.

The young man overcame this obstacle by turning to Rome and obtaining the permission for Fr. Guglielmo to accompany him.

They left. The good friar told his friend what he had to do. "There is only one way to speak to P. Pio. Firstly confess to him. Only afterwards you may talk about your financial situation. You must be brief, very brief."

"I understand", replied the young man." I will certainly confess and then I'll say: "Father I'm up to my ears in debt. I'm drowning".

When they arrived at San Giovanni Rotondo the contractor booked a confession which he made a few days later. When he received absolution he said to P. Pio what he had planned to say: "Father I'm drowning in debt".

The Saint put his hand in the man's shirt collar, loosened his tie and smilingly said " No, look I don't see you drowning".

The two pilgrims left for Romagna. The young man felt reassured and waited for things to change and they did. In a few months he was out of trouble.[35]

6. Every year Marietta Rosano from Cardito (NA) went up to San Giovanni Rotondo to say thank you to P. Pio and ask him once more for his help, which was never missing.

In 1950, she found herself in deep despair: she was alone without even the comfort of her parents. She absolutely needed to speak with a Saint, because, as she herself says, "Only saints can help in these cases".

---

[35] Fr. Gulielmo Gattani, Capuchin friar, Faenza (RA) 14.5.1998.

She thought of P. Pio and in order to get the money for the trip she had to sell a ring.

She went to the Gargano, waited eight days and finally was able to confess to him.

After receiving absolution, she did not know where to start talking about her problems. She froze, when the Padre said to her: "Come nearer!".

The penitent obeyed him. P. Pio took her hand and touching her fingertips, starting from her thumb, said: "You are in court because your husband has cheated on you and left you. You will not make up because he will not come back. However, you will always have your daily bread. Our Lady is near you and prays for you".

Marietta added: "You too, is that true?"

The Padre nodded his head in agreement.

I went away, ended Marietta, but even though I clearly realized my life would not be easy, I felt great peace within my heart.

I went back home and set to work, embroidering and sewing. I still do now even though I am 92 years old. My eyesight has always been good with their help, those in Heaven".[36]

Between the two bramble rows

To enter in the rays of action of the Padre's heart, it was not necessary to go to his confessional to let him know one's problems. It was enough to wait for him to pass by within the friary when carrying out his sacred duties, submerged in the daily crowds. He looked like a meek and mild little lamb crossing a

---

[36]   Marietta Rosano San Giovanni Rotondo 20.8.2005

narrow path full of bramble bushes, leaving traces of his fleece and drops of blood.

Sometimes, as soon as he came out of the confessional, the crowd threw themselves upon him so boisterously they frightened him: "Take it easy, relax! You look like a pack of hungry wolves!", he once said.[37]

Despite the noisy voices and the confusion, P. Pio perceived invocations and cries for help. He managed even with a few words to reassure and comfort souls. Therefore, it was that as the Saint went slowly by you could hear him say: "Yes", "All right", "No".

One day in the middle of the a racket, a woman's voice could be heard above the others. She waving a photo said: "Father, can I hope?". The Padre turning to where she was, said, "Yes, you can hope".[38]

The most common answer you could hear from the Saint's lips were: "I'll pray". Once Fr. Eusebio Notte asked him: "Spiritual Father, you told a woman you would pray for her.

But what exactly are you going to pray for?"

P. Pio said, "God knows that persons needs. I am only keeping my promise to remind Him".[39]

That the promised prayers were heard in Heaven is demonstrated by Anna Pugliese's testimony.

At the beginning of the sixties, she went from Cerignola to San Giovanni Rotondo, hoping to get close to P. Pio to ask him to pray for her sick father. He was still quite young, just over fifty, and after accurate medical examinations he had been di-

---

[37] Testimony received by a woman in confession, San Giovanni Rotondo, 24.6.1997.

[38] Anna Baroni, Chiavari 8.12.1994.

[39] Fr. Eusebio Notte, Morcone 17.8.1994.

agnosed with a prostatic hypertrophy and needed surgery.

He was very worried as he was the only breadwinner in the family.

Anna went to church hoping she could catch the Padre's eyes as he left the confessional going back to the friary.

At last the Saint started to move and she found herself in the middle of many imploring voices: "Father, my husband is ill, …Father my daughter has to do exams, …Father, I have to do an important test for a job …". She thought to herself; I will only say: "P. Pio, pray for my dad". She did so when he was near her.

The Saint stopped and asked her: "And who is your father?".

"Vincenzo Pugliese", answered Anna.

And P. Pio: "Very well"

The young girl went home full of hope.

After a few days, Vincenzo was admitted to hospital for the operation. On the morning of the operation, when he was ready to be taken to theatre the surgeon going to his bedside said: "Really I would like to see the patient again before I operate."

He examined him carefully and then to the surprise of all declared: "There is no need to operate".

Vincenzo himself was amazed at the professor's words, he could hardly believe them. The doctor a little annoyed but also amused said,

"You have a hypertrophy in your nose. Would you like me to operate on your nose?"

Vincenzo was discharged. He went home and had no further trouble.[40]

---

[40]   Anna Pugliese in Colangione, San Giovanni Rotondo 23.06.2005.

Amongst the people who crowed around the Padre's pathway, when he finished confessing there were always many mothers, they were always asking him to pray for their children.

1. One day Concepita Alfarana from Fasano and her husband waited in the cloister. As soon as the Saint popped out of the sacristy she shouted: "Father, we have brought Agata, our little girl who has been cured. We have come to thank you!".

P. Pio to the great joy of her parents, took the little girl in his arms and hugging her said: "Thank the Eternal Father and always pray!".

Agata's little story is told in a few lines. Her mother tells us: "I was desperate. In 1951, my daughter walked with a limp. I came to San Giovanni Rotondo and confessed to P. Pio. As soon as he opened the confessional grate, I immediately told him of this great sorrow. But he answered; "First think about confession".

I could not say a word and then he said: "You told a lie which has caused you problems".

"I don't remember, Father", I answered.

"I remember", added the Saint.

Then he told me not to be jealous of my husband and when confession was over, he asked me about my daughter. He listened to all I had to say and at the end, he advised me to take her to be seen.

She had a plaster cast but after nine months, there was no improvement. We took her to Bari to see Prof. Casucci, who noted that one leg was a few centimeters shorter than the other was. He advised that she be admitted for an operation.

I was disheartened and discouraged, but because of this, my faith was strengthened. I beseeched P. Pio with all my strength and he reassured me in a dream. After a few days, the little girl started to walk properly".[41]

2. A mother had gone to San Giovanni Rotondo with her sick daughter to ask the Saint for help. However, she did not have the chance to speak to him. She was only able to stand in the cloister corridor where he passed by.

When P. Pio appeared, all the women expressed their anxieties and problems. She stayed where she was and through her eyes, expressed the pain in her heart. The Padre stopped near her, caressed the little girl and said: "Go home and be at peace". And the little girl was cured.[42]

3. Amongst my memories is this note.

"27th August 1965. After the evening Mass, Fr. Giovanni Sammarone from Trivento introduced a relative of our confrère Benedetto Morrrone from Jelsi to the Padre. She asked him to put her five children under his protection.

"I've already got my five nails, do you want to give me these as well?", asked the Saint.

That mother, confident and forward replied: "These five nails I want to take, as long as you will protect my children".

P. Pio being benevolent but realistic answered: "Yes, Yes! You cannot even take your own…However that does not mean I will not think about them!".[43]

Some people did not even attempt to speak to the holy friar, they gave him letters with the problems and worries which had

---

[41]   Concepita Alfarano in Crofano, Fasano, (BR) 30.4.1991.

[42]   The little girl who was then a woman gave the testimony in confession. I did not ask her name. San Giovanni Rotondo 7.10.1999.

[43]   Personal diary.

caused them to go up to San Giovanni Rotondo. They certainly did not expect an answer. Once a man standing near me after delivering an envelope for the Padre, said to me: "It is enough that our worries have touched P. Pio". This was authentic faith. That was not deluded.

That the messages given to him by people in need did not lie idle is told to us by the Padre himself. Let us quote the San Giovanni Rotondo Friary Chronicle.

"One day Fr. Ruggero Di Maio from S. Elia a Pianisi, sacristan, on seeing many people giving P. Pio letters as he struggled through the crowd who thronged around him asked: "Spiritual Father, how do you deal with all these letters?", he was almost saying he wouldn't even have had time to open them.

P. Pio, sadly touching his heart, answered: "Look here they all pass; all in my heart."[44]

The Padre really put all the troubles, shown to him in that way, in his heart.

A woman traveling by train met a woman who was going to San Giovanni Rotondo to confess to P. Pio. She looked at her enviously and asked: "Could you take a message to that holy man for me?".

When the answer was yes, she ripped a piece of paper from a newspaper and wrote: "P. Pio pray for a mother of three who has to go in a sanatorium".

The two women never met again, but that sick mother never went to the sanatorium and is still alive today.[45]

---

[44] Chronicle…, f. 451: 4 August 1957.
[45] This testimony is from Masina Podda, ex minister of the Franciscan Third Order, who spoke to the miraculously healed woman; Oristano 22.4.1999.

There were those who did not even have the privilege to get close to the Padre when he went through the church or the friary. They joined the people who stood on the lawn opposite the Saint's little window. They wished to greet him and ask his blessing at certain times of the day.

The Padre thought of them too. Although he was sick and unable to go down into church either to say Mass or hear confession, how many times on hearing, the pilgrims shout their greetings or cries for help, he said: "They come from afar, they come to ask a little comfort and I can do nothing for them!".

Serena Sorcinelli from Mondolfo (Pesaro) is sure that one day the Padre at San Giovanni Rotondo greeted her and her friend in bilocation.

She says: "In November 1960 or 1961 a doctor called Aurelia and I, as we had to leave San Giovanni Rotondo, went underneath the Padre's window to receive a blessing from him when he appeared before resting in the afternoon. We had just waved to him and we went in the cloister corridor waiting for the bus, when the friary door opened and the holy friar appeared in the doorway.

It was a young P. Pio with a new habit. He was infinitely beautiful and surrounded by an aura of perfume. As soon as I saw him I said: "Father, bless my children".

And he, after making the sign of the cross over us, said; "Go in peace". And closed the door. It was 13-00 exactly.

Whilst we were full of joy and surprise the doorkeeper friar said: "What are you doing here?"

"We have just seen P. Pio", we answered. "What do you mean P. Pio? The Padre is resting!". Said the friar and soon after locked the friary door."

We also knew that the Padre was in his cell. We had just seen him from the lawn, but the Saint wanted to greet us in person in this amazing way, because we had not been able to confide our worries to him.[46]

Even Giovanna of Savoia, Vittorio Emanuele III's daughter, through marriage Giovanna of Bulgaria was one of the many people who had gone to San Giovanni Rotondo to tell her worries to P. Pio. Of course, she had the privilege of a private meeting, as is suitable for a queen.

The Padre as he went down the steps of the inside staircase to reach her and her lady-in-waiting, who were waiting for him in the old sacristy said: "I have come to gather the worries of one and all".

The queen thanked him on 21st January 1966.[47]

Sorrow of the Padre for not being able to soothe all pains

Between 1957-1958, the Neapolitan actress Titina De Filippo came to San Giovanni Rotondo. After being introduced to Fr. Pellegrino by an acquaintance she told him: "I am not very well and I would like to ask P. Pio to say a prayer and bless me".

This confrere of ours, who was keen on Neapolitan comedy could not believe he had the chance to make the artist's dream come true. He told her to wait in the small cloister, then went to the Padre to ask him if he could go down into the cloister to meet Titina.

P. Pio noted the warmth and interest with which the request was made and said: "I will come because I know your friend is

---

[46] Serena Sorcinelli, San Giovanni Rotondo 13.11.1996.

[47] I quaderni della Casa Sollievo della Sofferenza, n.24 June 2002, 25-26.

ill, as I am. I am always ready to be in sympathy with the suffering that unites men, never with those that separates them".[48]

Fr. Pellegrino describes the moving meeting.

"P. Pio with a gentle gaze, calmly scrutinized Titina for a second. He looked at her not as if he was seeing her for the first time but as if she was an old friend; and clearly wishing to increase the joy of faith within the pilgrim's heart, he happily gave her a heavenly smile. It was something he thought she would find pleasing and reassuring. Titina, feeling moved changed her expression immediately. She was no longer sad but smiling. It was as if she had received a peremptory order to distance every fear, and had carried it out perfectly. When she asked for his prayers, P. Pio full of understanding and compassion, told her simply and convincingly that from that moment onwards, she could count on his prayers.

Titina was genuinely grateful. Her joy was tinged with sadness knowing how ill she was, but sweetened by hope.

P. Pio affectionately put his gloved hand on her head. Titina was happy to put her soul into his hands. She listened flattered and devoted to the words of comfort the wise cordial friar said. She was happy for what she had received and to contemplate him as the dearest person in the world. She said nothing more.

But then thinking the sweet meeting had been too short because she had not kissed his hand, she stretched her hands towards him... P. Pio turned back and let the actress kiss his hand more than once. It was as if both of them were about to leave and were saying goodbye for the last time.

---

[48] Fr. Pellegrino Funicelli, Sofferenze firmate da Padre Pio, in Voce di Padre Pio, June 1976,14.

P. Pio blessed her again and as he went away, he turned back three times to wave goodbye and smile.

When he was alone with me, after going through the door, first he dried with his blue handkerchief, a trickle of blood gushing from his glove along the index finger of his left hand.

He was very moved and said the following prayer:

" I will not rebel against it my Lord.
But I'm sure You will agree with me
that it is a little too bitter
to not be able to express with deeds
to a poor sick woman
the sentiment of generosity
You yourself have put in my heart.
Certainly
I can't give anything to anybody
if I don't receive it from You first.
And this situation, because of Love or because I must,
I accept with humility.
But You make me suffer
not because You don't give to me
but because You don't enable me
to give something neither to You not to others.
However, Thy will be done my Lord".[49]

Fr. Pellegrino understood that P. Pio had not been able to snatch a cure for Titina from God's hands. He grumbled bitterly. The Padre calmly but severely said: "You can not force God's will past a certain point. I do not give graces. I am not even a Saint. I offer all the sufferings of my life, without ex-

[49] Fr Pellegrino Funicelli, *Non mi ribello, Signore*, in Voce di Padre Pio, September 1976, 11.

ceptions, for others and for your friend. I offer them to God. What else could I have done?".

But however, seeing that his confrère seemed like a young crazy foal he reprimanded: "Facing any sufferance the feelings of sympathy or antipathy should disappear and be replaced by those of compassion and love".

Fr. Pellegrino admitted that as well as solidarity, he also felt great affection for Titina. P. Pio although he had sadness in his heart, suggested: "It would be much better if you overcame your feeling of sympathy and affection, to see in her the millions of people suffering all over the world. In that way love does not diminish but grows and becomes perfect".[50]

A few years later, in 1963, Fr. Pellegrino heard the sad news of Titina De Filippo's death. When he told P. Pio he added that he would go and lay a flower from the friary garden on her grave when he was able to.

The Padre was moved and said to him: "The flower on that grave has already bloomed. You would be better saying a Mass for her". But when Fr. Pellegrino assured him he had already said a mass, he smiled and said: "Well then, if you really want to go and visit that grave take at least two flowers; one for you and one for me".[51]

3. The Padre calls

If the mission of the Padre, as his Spiritual father Benedetto Nardella had told him, was that of "co-redeeming", that

---

[50] FR. PELLEGRINO FUNICELLI, *I buoni ladroni*, in Voce di Padre Pio, October 1976,9.

[51] FR. PELLEGRINO FUNICELLI, Fiori sbocciati nell'orto del convento, in Voce di Padre Pio, April 1977, 13.

is joining Jesus to save souls, the Saint needed to necessarily imitate the Master in looking for the souls.

A series of testimonies, of which we can give only a small part, let us see how the Holy Spirit allowed his servant to carry out this task, even though he remained within the Friary walls.

Entrusting the message to friends and relations

1. Ippolito Lucchesi had accompanied his mother, who wished to confess to P. Pio, to San Giovanni Rotondo, and without even putting a foot in church, he had returned to Florence.

We know that even with the wait for a booking a fortnight was the usual time women waited to obtain a confession with the Padre. However after some months the woman was still on the Gargano near to her holy confessor. She was under his Spiritual direction and united to him in prayer.

Ippolito started to demand that she came home. She kept finding excuses and putting off her return to the family. One day her son wanted a full explanation as to what was happening. His mother told him what P. Pio had said to her: " Until your three children don't come here, you won't go back to your home town". The woman had not spoken of her children, or how many she had.

The first to make a move was Ippolito, the most instinctive and extrovert. However when he followed his mother's suggestion and went to confession, the Padre looked at him and said: "Where have you been up to now, in the jungle? Clear off!".

Despite this unwelcoming behaviour the penitent did not lose heart.

He returned to San Giovanni Rotondo soon after. He went to confession and this time the Padre started asking him some questions. However he was far away from what the Padre expected him to be. He had lived many years without God. He was not ready to receive Grace. Once more he was forced to leave without absolution.

However the friar with the wounded hands had already won his heart. Ippolito returned to Florence and changed his life style to the astonishment of his family and friends. He went down once more to Puglia. The Padre examined him carefully about his obedience to God's laws, finally he received absolution.[52]

2. The Lord let P. Pio know the needs of unknown souls who lived far away.

One day, after hearing a woman's confession he said to her: "Let your niece come and see me".

As the young girl lived in a town in the North of Italy, her aunt telephoned her. The girl came to San Giovanni Rotondo and entered the church. P. Pio called her whilst she was in the middle of some people. Someone said: "Look how P. Pio calls the girls!".

This gossip was referred to P. Pio who casually replied: "They will forget it".[53]

3. Caterina Mo, a worker at the knitwear factory Boglietti of Biella was called by the Padre in a special way. The Saint had said to a woman from Milan, when he had finished speaking to her: "Send someone to me". And she immediately thought of

---

[52] Ippolito Lucchesi, San Giovanni Rotondo 27.9.1994.
[53] This episoded was narrated by Pia Soldati; *Notes...*, San Giovanni Rotondo 19.5.1993.

her friend Caterina, who was very surprised at the proposal to go and meet the friar with stigmata.

She had never heard of P. Pio and no idea where San Giovanni Rotondo was. When she went to a travel agency to get some information, the clerk said: "But where do you want to go, a little woman like you?".

The price of a ticket, 7000 lire did not help either. It was an impossible price for her to pay. Every morning as she made her journey to work from Ponderano, where she lived, to Biella, about four or five kilometers away, she repeated to herself: "Seven thousand lire, seven thousand lire!".

The chance that she could meet P. Pio grew fainter.

Caterina every so often went to visit the Countess Rivelli of Biella. One day the countess gave her a closed envelope and said: "Take this and use it when you need it". When she returned to Ponderano she opened the envelope and to her amazement found exactly 7000 lire. Her thought went quickly to P. Pio. She bought her ticket and left.

A few days after arriving at San Giovanni Rotondo she had the chance to confess to the Padre. He on opening the confessional grate said: "Seven thousand lire, seven thousand lire! It took you long enough to decide to come, didn't it !?".

The conversation she had with the Saint was so gratifying for this simple good hearted woman, that as she was leaving she spontaneously said rather sadly: "Father, I'll say goodbye now as I won't ever come again". But the Saint quickly added: "No, no. You will come again many times and you'll bring lots of people with you" .

And so it was. In a few years she went down to San Giovanni Rotondo a good three times, and never on her own. It was at the end of the forties when travelling was not very easy. The Padre was very fond of Caterina.

Her travelling companions noted how Caterina communicated with P. Pio during Mass. He replied with signs of agreement to what she asked for. Usually prayers for other people.

Once, on the morning of her departure for Biella, the Padre did something particular. He greeted her by giving her a tap on the head with the communion plate.

(The little plate is used by the faithful to stop the host from falling.) He did this after giving her communion.

In another occasion Caterina, who didn't feel worthy to receive Jesus and fearing the Padre would skip her,[54] stayed standing, frozen to one spot. She did not approach the altar. When the Saint arrived near her, he took the little plate from the person kneeling at her side and gave it to her. Then he gave her communion.

When she was in Biella she couldn't contain the joy she had in meeting the Saint. She passed it on to others. Her conversation became a means of apostolate in the knitwear factory and elsewhere.

On her workbench next to images of the Sacred Heart and Our Lady she added a large photo of P. Pio. Every day, the fifteen workers who worked near her, recited the Rosary with her during their break.

One day something very strange happened. Caterina told her workmates that a mother, on hearing her son had died in Russia, wished to know from P. Pio if her son was at least safe in the other life. The answer she received from the Padre, unfortunately, was that he had got lost. On hearing this those present looked at P. Pio's photo on the workbench.

---

[54]   P. Pio when he was giving out communion did not always give every one the holy host. He gave it instead to the person who came next to them in the line of people on their knees at the alter rail.

To the amazement of all they saw a huge drop of blood, shaped like a thorn rounded at one side and sharp at the other, appear on P. Pio's forehead. Caterina commented: "Look how much sufferance, evil and its consequences affect the Padre!"

However not everyone accepted Caterina's good work. One day as she was walking a woman started to make fun of her devotion to P. Pio. Caterina stayed silent. When the woman moved away, Caterina smelt an odour of sulphur.

On 15th January 1950 she was amongst the founders of the Prayer Group at Biella named " The Association of the Devoted to Crucified Jesus, Spiritual Children of P. Pio of Pietrelcina".

During a holy Mass that the Group celebrated 20th September, the anniversary of when P. Pio received the stigmata, Caterina said to the others: "The Padre is present".[55]

4. This is what happened to Paolo Nigro.

He received his degree in Humanities in 1936 and took a second degree in Philosophy in 1940. His thesis denied the existence of God.

He taught in high school spreading his ideas. His wife however was strong in her faith. Because she was an orphan she had been brought up and educated in a convent run by Carmelite nuns and she stayed there until she was twenty-two.

Paolo, when he was full of intellectual vigour and feeling fit, was struck by illness. He had a dry pleurisy that in the spring of 1950 brought him close to death; the doctors in fact had declared they could do nothing more for him.

One Saturday evening in April at ten o'clock, two men knocked at the door of his house in Taranto; they introduced

---

[55] Rosetta Cappio raspa, Biella 2.12.1999.

themselves: Otello Risaliti a warrant office in the Navy and
Carlo Lusardi. Paolo's wife Maria did not want to let them in
the house. She was alone with her two children and her seriously ill husband. He had had a high temperature of 105° F for
two weeks. At times he was delirious, and seemed at death's
door.

The two men insisted saying: "P. Pio sent us and we have to
say the rosary for someone who is seriously ill".

The poor woman, who had never heard of P. Pio was most
perplexed. She had a word with her sick husband who having
heard them speak of the rosary, gave his permission. Finally
she let them in.

We must say that a few years before, in 1946, Prof. Nigro
had slightly changed his opinion as an atheist. He had asked
to meet the Archbishop of Taranto, Mons Bernardi to whom
he had said he had had a kind of vision in which he saw Our
Lady's profile.

After this he started to go to Mass, even though he didn't
go regularly. Perhaps this was the reason he let two strangers,
who wanted to pray for him to the Blessed Virgin, come into
his house.

Santina, Paolo's daughter, who was a child at the time tells
us what happened: "I can see it as if it were yesterday. These
two men, Risaliti in his white uniform and Lusardi, both kneeling and devotedly saying the rosary.

However as they were praying, dad was restless and said
to mum: "Maria, send that hooded friar at the foot of the bed
away". Mum said nothing; she imagined that vision was due to
his high temperature".

Before leaving after finishing the rosary, the Padre's spiritual sons discreetly begged Maria to accept some money:" "It
is sent by P. Pio. You will need it next week to pay for your

husband's the journey from Taranto to San Giovanni Rotondo. The Padre wishes to see him. And for the medicines". About this particular point Santina explains: "It was as if P. Pio knew we had spent nearly all our money to buy penicillin which was very expensive at the time".

The following Monday, the sick man was much better. His temperature went down. The doctors were amazed. His health had improved so much that on Thursday, three days later, at 9.00 in the morning, Risaliti and Lusardi came to collect him and took him by taxi to Taranto station. In the evening they arrived at San Giovanni Rotondo, they, together with the convalescent, took lodgings in a little white house on the right, going up the road leading to the friary.

The next day, Friday, they took him to the sacristy where P. Pio was confessing men. At the end of the confessions, P. Pio came out from the curtain, which hid him from view of onlookers.

"Dad" said Santina, recognized in him "the friar" who the previous Saturday he had seen at the foot of the bed whilst the the rosary was being said. He went up to him and threw himself on his knees, crying.

The Padre helped him up holding his wrists and said in dialect: "If you cry, I won't come to your house any more".

The next day dad confessed to the Saint, who put him back in God's grace and accepted him as a spiritual son. He became a different person. He went to Mass every day and took part in the holy communion.

The Padre continued to be near him in those first steps into a new life. He came to visit him at home. During his convalescence dad sometimes said to me: "Santina, P. Pio is putting his hand on your head".

I have often seen him crying because of his past misbelieve. He tried to make up for it by taking many people to P. Pio, and to God". [56]

P. Pio calls from the confessional

1. Mrs Rachele Ricciardi of San Giovanni Rotondo, wished to confess to the Padre. As she had a large family to look after, she had to find a moment when she wasn't busy. Stealing a moment from her chores she went up to the friary and joined the queue in front of the confessional. It was before there were booked tickets. People were expected naturally to wait their turn. However that morning it seemed as if her turn would never come.

She waited and waited. Then she waited a little more but her thoughts raced to the jobs she had to do at home. She decided that she had to go back home, when she saw P. Pio move the confessional curtain and say to the surrounding women: "Let that women pass".

So she managed to confess.[57]

2. Sometimes, the Padre interrupted hearing confession, to bring people who were pausing in church, near to him. We report a testimony in which one can see how the Saint comforted and bound a spiritual daughter to him for all her life.

She recounts: "I was 18 when my mother took me to see P. Pio in 1950. She wanted to ask him to pray and intercede so that I may be cured. I was suffering from heavy continual hemorrhages. It is known that it was necessary to book to speak

---

[56]   Santina Nigro, San Giovanni Rotondo 10.05.2005.

[57]   Rachele Ricciardi, Campitello Matese (CB) 26.12.1998.

to the Padre. Whilst my mum and some other women were asking what they had to do to book, I went into church.

P. Pio was sitting in the confessional. At a certain point, he moved the curtain that hid him from the faithful and pointing at me said to Fr. Tarcisio Zullo from Cervinara: "Let that girl come here".

I went and kneeling before him, I said these actual words "I am one of Maria's daughters", then I added the reason why I had gone to San Giovanni Rotondo.

He put his hand on head and said: "Don't worry, don't worry". Whilst his words reached my ears, I felt something like a weight lie heavy on my head.

When the confessions were over, the Padre passed through the cloisters, where my mother and I were, amongst other women. When he saw me he said: "Are you still here? Go home and don't worry any more!"

I went home and within a few days the hemorrhages stopped. However, I have felt P. Pio's protection all my life. In difficult moments, his presence has almost been physical.

I married my husband and we really loved each other. However after many years of a happy marriage lived in the most beautiful love, he cheated on me for about ten years. I stayed in my place praying Our Lady and Padre Pio. During that dark period, my husband hated me and cursed Our Lady and the Padre, just because he knew they were mine.

We had two children. The first got caught up with drugs and needed prayers.

I dreamt of P. Pio. The first time I saw him running towards me in the countryside; the second time when my husband was ill with cancer.

I felt as if I was in the sacristy of a church. I was sitting on a bench. There was someone near me, who seemed very poor.

He looked like a tramp and he came closer and closer to me. I did not move not to upset him.

He had a friar's habit, but a hat covered his head. I bent down to look at his face. I recognized P. Pio. I said "Father!".

And he made an expression which seemed to say: "I can't do anything to help!". Soon after my husband died suffering as one on the cross".[58]

… Among the people in church: 1956

The Marquis of S. Elia, Maria Francesca Starabba (maiden name Arezzo), had a daughter, Maruzza who had heart problems and the family doctor in Palermo advised that she be examined by a well-known cardiologist from Rome. After a careful examination, she was diagnosed as having a heart murmur. In the illustrious doctor's opinion, the girl would not be able to marry nor have children.

A family friend suggested to the extremely worried mother, that she went to see P. Pio. The friend knew Dr. Sanguinetti who had collaborated with P. Pio in the building of the Home for the Relief of Suffering. He offered to write a letter of presentation, which would make it easier for her to meet the Padre.

Mrs Starabba accepted his offer of help and left for the Gargano. When she arrived in front of the Capuchin friary, she did not look for anyone but went straight into church. Whilst P. Pio was busy confessing. She mingled among the crowd waiting for the holy friar to pass by on his way back to the friary.

---

[58]   This testimony was given in Genova 22.4.1995. The person wishes to remain anonymous.

When the Padre came out of the confessional, she heard the cries of supplication that many mothers made to the man of God. They all wanted him to intercede for them. She prayed in her heart for her daughter.

Then she saw that P. Pio with a wave of his hand was calling her. She despite the throng of people made her way to him and the Padre said to her: "Don't worry; your daughter does not have anything. She can get married and have children".

Her daughter got married and had children as P. Pio said she would.[59]

...From the Church Square

1. Sister Assunta (Felicia) Marchesano, born in Portocannone (CB) 23rd January 1936, after a course of spiritual exercises, with the theme from the Gospel "*They dropped their nets immediately, and followed him*" (MK 1, 18), began to think about becoming a nun. She was 12 years old, but as time went by the conviction that she had been called to embrace the religious life became stronger and stronger. To her father who wanted to take her into the fields with to work on the land, her mother used to repeat: "She is not cut out to be work on the land".

But he replied "You just let her win you over."

And she answered: "Every one should be able to choose their own life".

Felicia also had a brother and a sister who also caused problems. They were on their father's side and said "Mum always sticks up for her."

---

[59]   Fr. Giovanni Meli, Vittoria 11.6.1998.

One day some Franciscan nuns came to the farm asking for charity for some orphans.

The good man gave what he was able to, but when the nuns left he said, "I'll help them though we've no food but I won't send my daughter, to beg like a wretch".

In 1953 her parents, to try and dissuade her from her idea and to keep her away from her home town friends who encouraged her choice, sent her to stay with her Godmother who lived in a railway house on the line Foggia- S. Severo.

One day the woman suggested going San Giovanni Rotondo to see P. Pio: she had been thinking of going for a while. The girl agreed.

When they arrived at the little square in front of the Friary, they saw a rather thin little friar. He came out of the friary door and said to the Godmother: "Are you Giuseppina, from the first railway house of Foggia?".

When she said she was the friar told her: "P. Pio is waiting for you, but first he wishes to speak to the girl who wants to become a nun."

The woman was very surprised and turned to her Goddaughter and said: "Felicetta, if you had an appointment with P. Pio you could have told me!".

The girl assured her that she did not even know the Padre.

The friar let the girl wait in the first room of the cloister corridor. After a while, P. Pio arrived and said: "At last you have arrived. I have been waiting for you for a long time".

As the girl protested that she had never seen him before, the Saint said: "You don't know me but I have known you for a long time". He let her take a seat and began confession.

At the end he said: "You will become a nun, despite the opposition of your father and your brother. However They will not speak to you for thirty years. You will also have a moment of great difficulty in your life in the community. In spite of this, with willpower you will overcome all. You have a will of iron. You must pray, pray and pray. You have to pray a lot because there are always tests in the religious life. You must not be discouraged. After you reach forty years of age you will have to have a heart operation. But you will get over this too. Do not be afraid when you have the operation. You are strong. You will survive".

The young girl listened in amazement to all P. Pio said. She could hardly believe what she heard but when the events began to come true she remembered the words the Saint had said.

Felicia returned to Foggia and stayed with her Godmother for another two months. Then she returned home. She told her father of her meeting with P. Pio and of her firm decision to become a nun.

Her father showed no further resistance to her plan; he only said: "If it is God will, so be it".

So Felicia was free to enter in the congregation of her choice on 18th September 1995. She took her religious habit in March 1956. After a year and half as a novice, she made her vows and took the name of Sister Assunta.[60]

2. Brother Mario Largher from Val di Cembra (TN) took part in the first pilgrimage to Lourdes, organized by the Caritas from Florence. During the trip, a stretcher bearer asked him if he was a Capuchin friar.

When he was given an affirmative answer he told him: "I met P. Pio, but in an unusual way. My friend and I who worked for the railways used to make fun of all we heard about P. Pio, and those who told us about him. On one of our days off, we

---

[60] Sister Assunta Marchesano, Pescara 3.5.2001.

decided to take a trip to San Giovanni Rotondo, because being railwaymen we didn't have to pay . We decided to go just for curiosity. When we arrived, we went into church but we did not see P. Pio as he had just retired after finishing confession.

Whilst we were in the square in front of the church, amidst the people there, a friar came out and asked: Are there two railway workers here from Trento?"

We felt as if we had been struck by lightening. We went forwards. "P. Pio wishes to see you" he said.

He let us enter into a private part of the cloisters where we met P. Pio. From that moment our lives changed radically".

Brother Mario, who told us this, ended saying: "That stretcher bearer did not say anything else, nor did he mention what P. Pio could have said to them. He just let me understand that from being an atheist he had become a spiritual son of the Saint".[61]

3. Gina Deiana tells us.

"Two months before the date fixed for my wedding day, my fiancée got rid of me, by leaving a calling card with the words: "You are free". He never came to see or speak to me again. I sunk into a deep depression, all was anguish and blackness. I cried day and night and my parents did not know what to do to make me feel better.

One day I read in a magazine that a Holy Saint who comforted and cured lived in the South of Italy. I decided to go to see him.

In October 1952, together with an Aunt I left from Genova

---

[61]   Brother Mario Largher, capuchin friar, Trento 29.7.1997.

and after two days we arrived in San Giovanni Rotondo.

We lodged in the only existing hotel, S. Maria delle Grazie. After supper the owner said: "If you would like to go to P. Pio's Mass, I will call you at 3 am".

Even though we were tired, we accepted her kind proposal. We slept little less than four hours.

In the morning, I saw the Padre for the first time.

Since we had taken some flowers with us after breakfast we went back to the church; but as I was climbing the steps of the little square, a woman came up to me, Angelina Serritelli, she said: "You are the love sick girl, aren't you?".

"And how do you know about me? "I asked.

"P. Pio sent me and he said you have to stay here and go and see him."

"But we haven't got a bank here that can give us any money!"

"I will lend you some."

"But you don't know me, how can you trust me?".

"This is something you must not worry about"

I have no idea what indication P. Pio could have given that comforting messenger, to find me. I had the feeling I had found myself in a new world, an Earthly Paradise".

The day after I had the chance to see the Holy Friar close up. When he looked at me with his big eyes, I said to myself: "But this is Jesus!".

I phoned home to tell my mum I was staying longer than planned. I remember that when she objected I explained: "Mum, I have the impression I have arrived in Heaven". She answered: "This one has gone crazy!".

Finally, I was able to confess to the Padre. The first thing I said was: "Because I felt so sad and down after being abandoned by my fiancée, I stopped taking communion. You however, know that I have done nothing wrong."

That unique confessor calmed me down, he told me to relax and not think about what had happened because "that man" was a "scoundrel and he had another woman". I continued my confession, admitting that sometimes I was rude when answering my mother.

"Yes, but you feel sorry afterwards, don't you?" he said.

He gave me absolution and peace returned to my heart. I passed by to kiss his hand and he gave me a little picture card of Lord Jesus: the Padre continued to amaze me! In my prayers, I loved to contemplate Jesus as he taught his disciples and the people around him. P. Pio had written on it: "Let Jesus be at the centre of all your aspirations".

When the day of our departure came nearer, the Padre gave us two orphans to take to an institution in Turin. We did so feeling privileged that he had entrusted us with this task.

When I returned to Genova, I wanted to meet my ex-fiancée despite the Padre's ban. I went with a friend to what should have been my house. I waited in the waiting room and when it was my turn, I went in. He was surprised. I said: "I went to see P. Pio and he said that you are a scoundrel and you have another woman". He admitted it and added he was getting married in two months. I replied," You almost drove me to madness but P. Pio saved me and gave me back peace of mind".[62]

Gina became a spiritual daughter of P. Pio who looked after her soul for years. She often came down from Liguria. Then when she closed her business involved with selling flowers, she left Genova and moved to San Giovanni Rotondo where she still lives.

---

[62]   Gina Deiana, San Giovanni Rotondo 18.11.2004.

A rabid anticlerical, called in a dream, builds a church

Giovanni Bardazzi lived in Prato, not only away from God but also from all that had to do with God. In 1949 he dreamt of P. Pio who said to him: "I'm waiting for you at San Giovanni Rotondo". But he took no notice at all. Imagine if a friar could even slightly arise interest in a man like him!

After a few months, the Padre showed himself again, once more in a dream. He gave a command this time: "Now that's quite enough ! I'm waiting for you." Giovanni started to show signs of weakness in his attitude towards a certain reality that he had fought against and made fun of in the past.

His wife Ottavina often went in the evening to say the rosary with Mrs Demarista Parretti. Sometimes she asked her husband to accompany her but he repeated: "If you want you can go on your own to see that half fool". Once however, without objecting he went with his wife. As soon as he entered the house he heard the host who welcomed him say:" Why do you want to waste the good heart you have?". Giovanni confessed later that strangely enough the tone of the voice, which reached his ears, was not of a woman, but of that person he had seen in his dream.

He finally decided to make the journey to San Giovanni Rotondo, but how much sufferance it cost him !

He left on 6th April 1950 with his wife. His main wish was to see if P. Pio was the friar he had dreamt of, the one wearing half- gloves.

When he arrived at San Giovanni Rotondo, he went into church and straight into the sacristy where, as they had told him, he could see the friar at a certain time. He tried to mingle in with the men who were waiting, but without wishing to, he found himself on the front row.

As soon as the Padre came down the stairs and entered the room, he looked at Giovanni and said, "The troublesome sheep has arrived !". Then he went into church to confess the women.

Giovanni, left on his own asked how he could speak to the Padre. They told him the only way was to confess. He put his name on the list and prepared to wait his turn. After a few days his turn came.

He was called from the sacristy but as soon as he approached the confessional P. Pio did not even let him kneel down " Go away ! Go and confess, go to Mass and come back in two months", he said.

Giovanni went away with his soul rebelling. When he returned to Prato, to his amazement he felt obliged to obey. He went to mass every Sunday an unusual thing for him. However not to let his friends and people he knew see him he chose the church, Santa Maria delle Carceri, where every morning there was a mass for hunters at an early hour.

After two months, he punctually presented himself to the Padre. As soon as he saw him kneeling down the Saint asked: "Did you go to Mass?"

"Yes Father, I went early in the morning because I was ashamed".

"Go away. You are worse than before!", shouted the Saint.

After a few months, for the third time Giuseppe went down South to reach the Gargano and he went to confession. He confessed he had sworn sometimes and the Padre reproved him harshly. "You, said the penitent, are reproving me because I have sworn?! And what if I told you I am a communist ?"

" My son, it is not a question of politics. It is that you still have an unclean soul", replied the Saint and he sent him away.

Giovanni by this time was fascinated by the Padre and could not break away from him. For the fourth time he returned to San Giovanni Rotondo and thought of every way of being accepted by him as one of his spiritual children.

He heard that some people went to the cemetery to pray P. Pio's mother and father to be an intermediary between them and the Saint.

The day fixed for his confession he bought a candle. It was the first time in his life he had done so. When he arrived at the cemetery, he neared the grave of the lucky parents and said, "You know that I do not know how to pray. Please help me".

In the afternoon, he went to the sacristy. After a while, the Padre came down. Giovanni confessed and finally he was listened to. As a good Tuscan, he could not help but make a slight protest, "Father you made me suffer for a year to give me this blessed absolution."

"You were the hammering the nails in", dryly replied the Saint.

Giuseppe went home and changed his life completely.

The first thing he did was leave the communist party. The day he arrived at the club to give in his membership card, someone cried ironically: "Companions, what a stink ! Can't you all smell it ?".

Giovanni who wasn't the type to be fearful, replied quickly: "I can smell it too. How can you stand it in here?" To whose asked for an explanation about his change of heart he said: "I found God. Here there is no God".

He was made fun of and laughed at, but he remained true to his promises and faithful to the Padre.

P. Pio called Giovanni because there was a mission for him to carry out. In 1953 after, a confession, the Saint told him to leave his cloth business and start another job: "But Padre, that is the job I know how to do", protested Giovanni.

The Saint replied: "God closes one door and opens another".

Whilst he thought about how to change his business, Giovanni started to spend most of his weekends at San Giovanni Rotondo, taking people with him so that they could meet the Padre. Once he introduced a man to P. Pio who was looking for a partner for the recycling of motor oil. The Saint advised them to form a partnership.

They decided to buy some land to start the business. They thought about two sites. One in Santa Lucia, Prato and the other at Calenzano in a plot of land called, The Name of Jesus. When they asked the Padre which they should choose, he replied: "It is better to build at The Name of Jesus."

The business began, but there were lots of problems. One day Giovanni put so many bundles of wood under the boiler that when they lit, the fire started to worry him. He was inexperienced. He climbed up the ladder and saw the boiler was boiling in an alarming way. He got down as fast as he could and went back far back. Soon after some boiling oil spilled all over the room.

When he could finally step back inside, he was so angry he got P. Pio's picture and turned it around. Then as usual, he left to spend the weekend at San Giovanni Rotondo. The Padre, as soon as he saw him said: "I'm not very happy with my face against the wall".

After a while, Giovanni's partner decided to leave the business. Giovanni was left to do everything by himself.

One day the Padre asked him: "How many square meters is our factory?"

"A thousand meters, Father".

"Why? Weren't there more?", asked the Saint.

"Yes Father, there are 10,000 but we are already lucky to have taken 1000 at 50,000 lire a month".

"The Saint added: "Go on, take them all". The son obeyed and did as the Padre had advised.

Things started to go very well. So much so, that Giovanni managed to put a fair bit aside. He decided to invest the capital buying another business. Naturally, before doing so he asked the Padre for his advice. The answer he received was certainly not what he expected. "My son, you will make a church and a house for you".

Giovanni, was extremely surprised. It seemed an impossible task for him. He said to the Padre: "I will tell the priest to build the church". But the Saint added: "No the walls must be ours".

Once again the son obeyed, despite a certain opposition from his family. They did not believe that what he wanted to do was really part of the Padre's wishes and plans.

Soon after on the land he had bought, a chapel and a house arose, they were separated by a piece of land that the Bardazzi family made into a vegetable garden for their own needs.

In the meantime in that area a notable building development took place and what was once countryside became a large inhabited area. The Padre was interested and asked: "Do many people come to our little Church?".

"Yes, Father, there are so many they hardly all fit in".

The conversation seemed as it ended there but not long after, during a relaxing moment with the friars, in the garden, the Padre called his spiritual son to one side and said: "Giovanni, what are you doing with those cabbages and tomatoes? Enlarge the church !"

Poor Giovanni was unprepared for the Saint's proposal and

spent all evening pondering it. Things in the firm were not going extremely well. There were always bills to pay. The next Saturday he was at San Giovanni Rotondo again and of course spoke of his worries to P. Pio. The Saint quite naturally said: "You haven't got enough money? Well go and find some".

Giovanni had always done as the Padre had said and never made a mistake. Why should he doubt him now? He left heartened and sure, he was not alone in his latest venture. He thought of who he could go to and chose a rich industrialist of the area.

He went to the caretakers lodge. He was taken to see Mr. A. B. and without formally introducing himself or beating about the bush, he said: "I need two million".

The man looked at him in surprise and said " Do you think I have got "Salt and Tobacco shop written on my forehead? Explain yourself."

"I have come to ask you for a loan to enlarge the church P. Pio wanted built".

Mr A.B. jumped up from his chair and said severely: "Don't mention that holy name!"

But Giovanni stayed calm and said: "I name him, because I am telling the truth".

Now it was the rich man's turn to feel embarrassed: he knew the Padre and not long before he had personally made a donation for his hospital. He stayed silent for a minute and then proposed that he and Giovanni went together to San Giovanni Rotondo. He wanted to be sure that P. Pio was really involved in this matter.

The two left. When they arrived at the friary, they waited to meet the Padre who as soon as he saw them said to his spiritual son: "Oh Giovanni! When did you arrive?" and he embraced him". A.B. was frozen to the spot by that scene and realized that, the man whom he did not know, was well known to P. Pio.

Giovanni instead was in seventh heaven: the worries, regarding the debts he had to face, all disappeared. He presented his traveling companion to the Saint. P. Pio said to the guest: "You will give him the money without interest, which he will pay back, in time when he can".

Mr A. B. at that moment pulled out his chequebook and making Giovanni bend over, used his shoulders to write out a cheque of two million.

He gave him another million to give to the Padre later. That was for other works of charity. He also wished to have a private meeting with the Saint: He had an incurable leg illness and he wished to speak about it.

When Giovanni carried out A. B's wish, the Padre was amazed at that generous donation. He could hardly believe his eyes seeing all those "zeros" on the cheque; however, as to the benefactor's request he said: "Give the cheque back. Here, nobody can be bought". Then, because Giovanni insisted, he took the donation that could help the sick.

The day after the two pilgrims took their leave, P. Pio said goodbye and with the back of his hand tapped the troublesome leg of that man who was rich but very concerned about his health, saying to him: "Ah this leg, this leg!". From that moment, the leg problem disappeared.

Soon afterwards working to enlarge the little church which was given the same name as the shrine of San Giovanni Rotondo: Santa Maria delle Grazie (Our Lady of Grace), began. And Giovanni, who was big hearted and generous, donated to the diocese of Prato not only the church but also his house and all the land where his firm stood. Today that church which has become a parish church, has its own presbytery and ample rooms for various functions.

So that man who declared himself a communist and an atheist and whose plan once was, as he himself said, to "turn churches into stables and to cut priests into four", became, because of P. Pio's work, an instrument of God, an apostle of his Reign.

After the consecration of the church on 7th December 1960 by the Archbishop of Florence E. Florit, one day the Padre said to his spiritual son: "You have paid now with your money, later you yourself will have to pay. You will be slandered and betrayed by your dearest friends."

And so it was. "There is something behind it, some self interest," said his enemies and people who knew him. They were spiteful and abusive.

However Giovanni was a "new man", he feared nothing. He said: "My soul has turned upside down. Everything about me and around me has changed. Even the plants are different". His reference point was P. Pio and his words. In them he saw Jesus.

He loved his spiritual father above all, and when he saw him suffering he said: "I want to help you carry your pain".

But P. Pio replied: "No that is only for me."

He took many people by car to San Giovanni Rotondo. He did so that they too could benefit from that gift Heaven had conceded to earth.

And the Padre returned the affection that Giovanni showed by allowing him to become more familiar. The brother friars who lived with P. Pio knew that he willingly saw this spiritual son who, when at San Giovanni Rotondo, asked to spend as much time as possible with P. Pio and nobody objected.

On the contrary the father guardian, who sometimes in the past had been rather strict in allowing him to move freely, one day asked him a favour. Dr. Gugliemo Sanguinetti had died and the Padre was visibly upset for the loss of this man. Sanguinetti had been very involved in the realization of the Home for the Relief of Suffering. The Saint was not himself during recreation.

"Listen, said the Father superior to Giovanni, see if you can make P. Pio smile a little, we can't manage it".

The next evening when the brother friars and friends gathered around the Padre, Giovanni had the right to sit next to him.

P. Pio began to speak of his dearly departed friend: "My son", he said " you can't get fond of anyone, or the Lord takes them away", and with his hand he affectionately tapped Giovanni's leg.

The Saint made another comment and stroked Giovanni's knee; then a third reflection followed by the same affection gesture.

At this point Giovanni interrupted saying: "Father, don't let those "up there" see that you are very fond of me, otherwise they'll take me as well !"

Everyone burst out laughing, including P. Pio.

In one of the last recreations that Giovanni took part in, this affection son arrived a little late to put himself on the front row to enjoy the Padre's conversation. As he was no giant and therefore unable to see, he decided to go up to the first floor of the friary. He opened the window and from above, as if in a theatre box he was enjoying the scene below him, when P. Pio raised his eyes and said: "Giovanni, what are you doing up there?"

"Father, I am watching you, he replied, I hope to see you so closely in Heaven".

"No, there we will be much closer", assured the Saint.[63]

---

63   Ottavina Bardazzi, wife of Giovanni, Cadenzano (FI) 7.9.2001.